A–Z OF TRURO

PLACES - PEOPLE - HISTORY

John Husband

AMBERLEY

First published 2021

Amberley Publishing
The Hill, Stroud, Gloucestershire, GL5 4EP
www.amberley-books.com

ISBN 978 1 4456 9641 6 (print)
ISBN 978 1 4456 9642 3 (ebook)

British Library Cataloguing in Publication Data.
A catalogue record for this book is available from the British Library.

Typesetting by Aura Technology and Software Services, India. Printed in Great Britain.

Contents

Introduction

Sited at the confluence of the rivers Allen and Kenwyn, Truro is an ancient town but a young city. Between becoming Cornwall's first chartered town in 1130 to the laying of the foundation stone for the county's only cathedral in 1880, it has gone from a medieval market town to a thriving port, and as a stannary town grown rich on the proceeds of Cornwall's mines. Fine Georgian buildings changed the look of Truro from a provincial market town to a smaller version of Bath. Its street plan

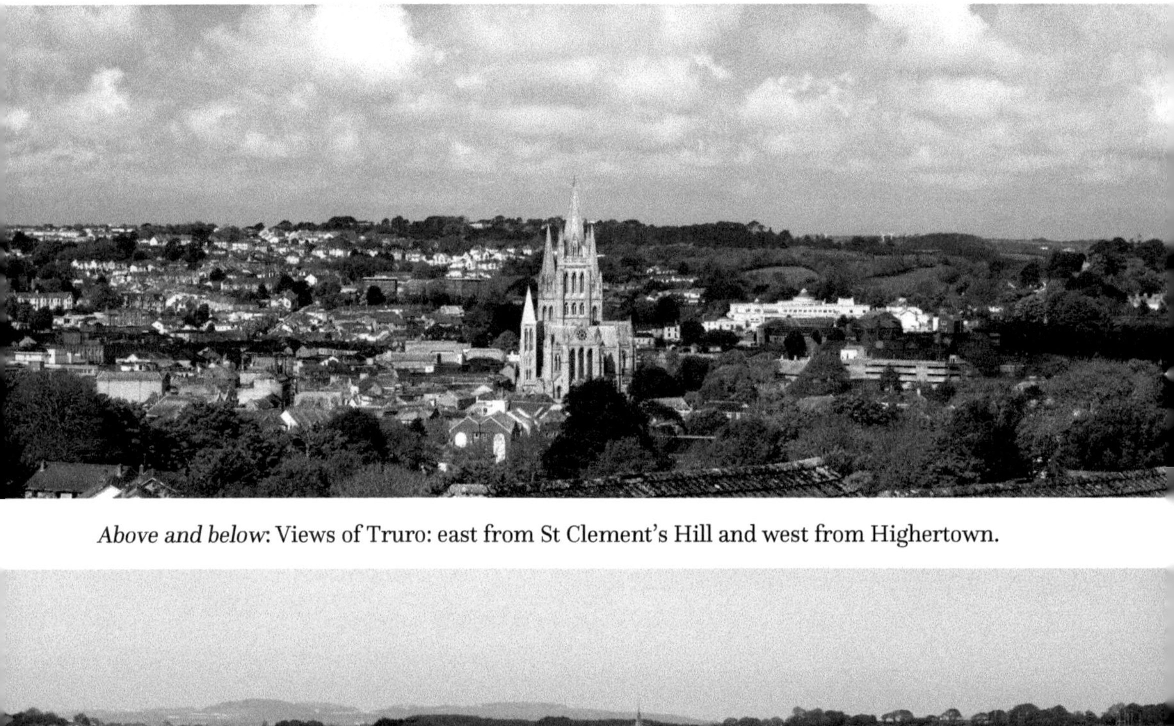

Above and below: Views of Truro: east from St Clement's Hill and west from Highertown.

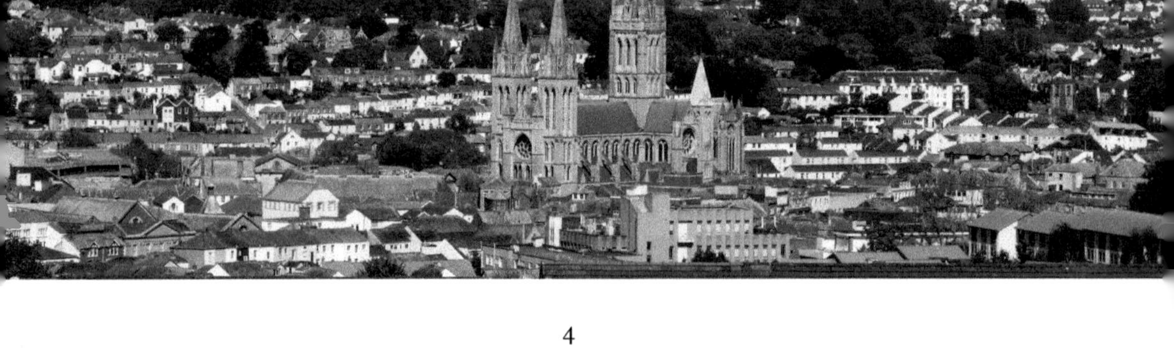

contains many narrow passageways or opes, probably dating from medieval times, and many of its interesting buildings still remain despite much modern development as befits Cornwall's premier legal, administrative and commercial centre. During the eighteenth and nineteenth centuries, Truro-born men sent their influence far and wide across the country and the world. The city's only Royal Academician, Henry Bone, practised his art in the capital, where the actor and comedian Samuel Foote also trod the boards, whilst Richard Lander led expeditions to West Africa and Thomas Keam became a highly respected Indian trader in the US, rubbing shoulders with politicians and presidents. For all its great and good, however, very few statues were erected to their memory, and there are no official blue plaques at all. Compared to today's equal opportunities society, nineteenth-century Truro was not so backward either. A former African slave ended up as a leading society musician in the town, a deaf-mute architect designed many of its best buildings, and a confectioner's daughter graduated from Cambridge and became a member of the British Astronomical Society. It has also made its contribution to twentieth-century culture: did you know that the City Hall was the location for the first ever appearance of a band named *Queen*? Or that without Annie 'Spitfire' Penrose, the Battle of Britain would have been won by a fighter plane called the *Shrew*?

When its shipping trade was eventually stolen by Falmouth, much closer to the sea, the river silted up and now only small boats can reach the Town Quay, and then only at high tide. By the first years of the twentieth century two developments had changed the look of the town forever. The arrival of the railway in the middle of the century brought the massive sixteen-arched viaduct, 1,300 feet long, which stretches across the panorama of the city from east to west across the valley of the Allen. In front of it rise the three spires of the country's first Anglican cathedral to be built since St Paul's. A smaller bell tower is roofed in Cornish copper, now oxidised green, enhancing the city with a Gothic building which could have come straight from Normandy.

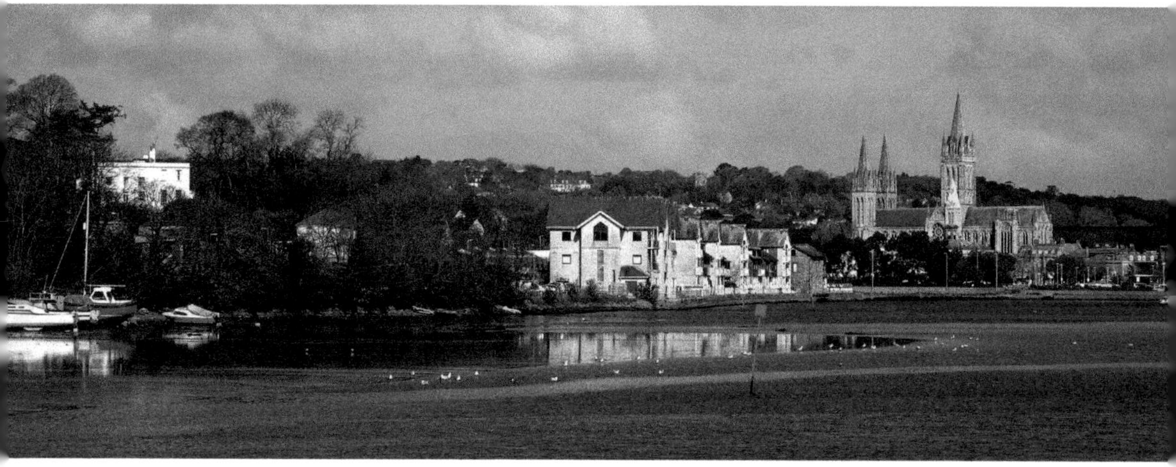

Newham and the cathedral from Boscawen Park.

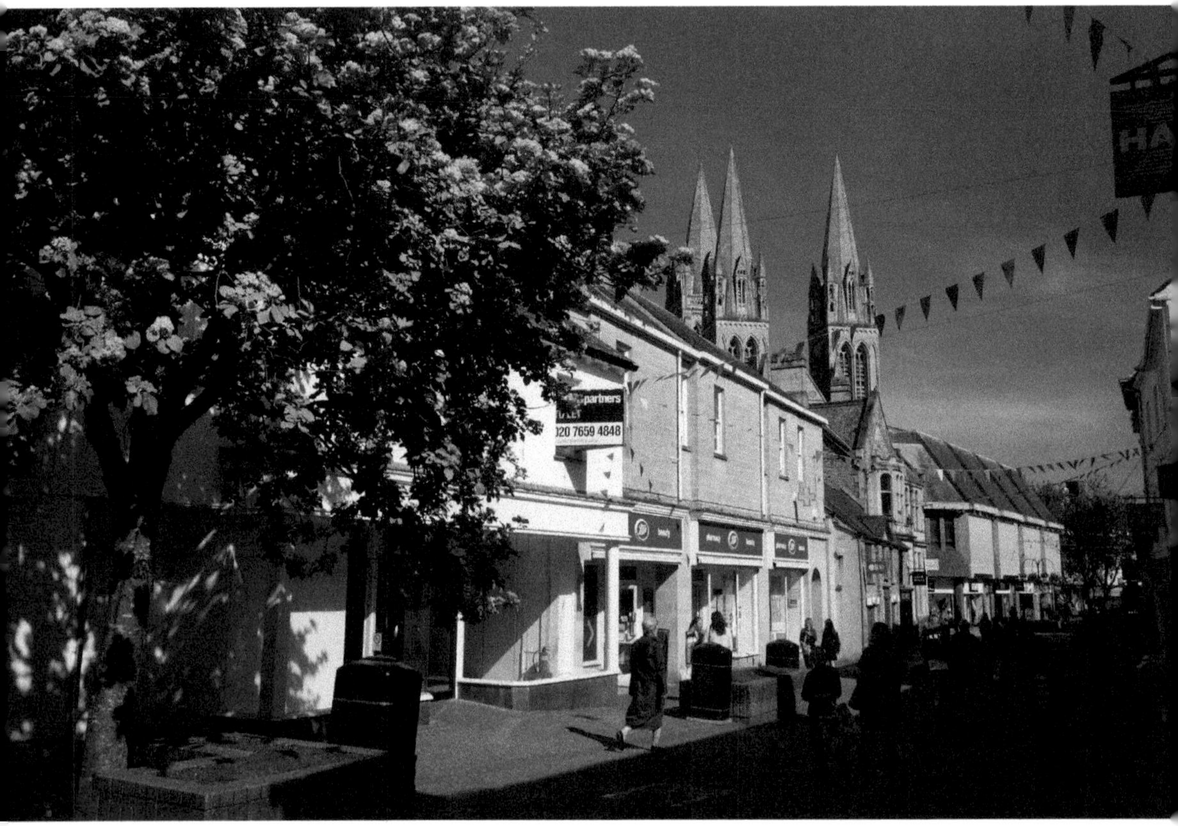

Pydar Street.

Truro is a compact city, smaller in fact than the county's largest towns. Its population is just over 20,000, less than St Austell, Falmouth or Camborne. Its location in a river valley means that it is surrounded by high ground, which affords some iconic views of the city, dominated from all directions by the spires of the cathedral. Whether from Highertown in the west, Kenwyn to the north or St Clement's Hill to the east, today it is difficult to imagine the city without these iconic structures. There are also plenty of nature trails and parks in which to relax, namely the Newham Trail, Daubuz Moor, and the award-winning Victoria Gardens and Boscawen Park. The attractive hamlets of Idless, Malpas, St Clements and Calenick all lie within 2 miles of the city.

A

River Allen

The name Truro is thought to be derived from the Cornish *tri veru* meaning 'three rivers'. One of these, the River Allen, rises near the village named after it and flows through the Idless valley and through the city to join the River Kenwyn, which then goes on to become the Truro River. The third river is the Glasteinan, which is today

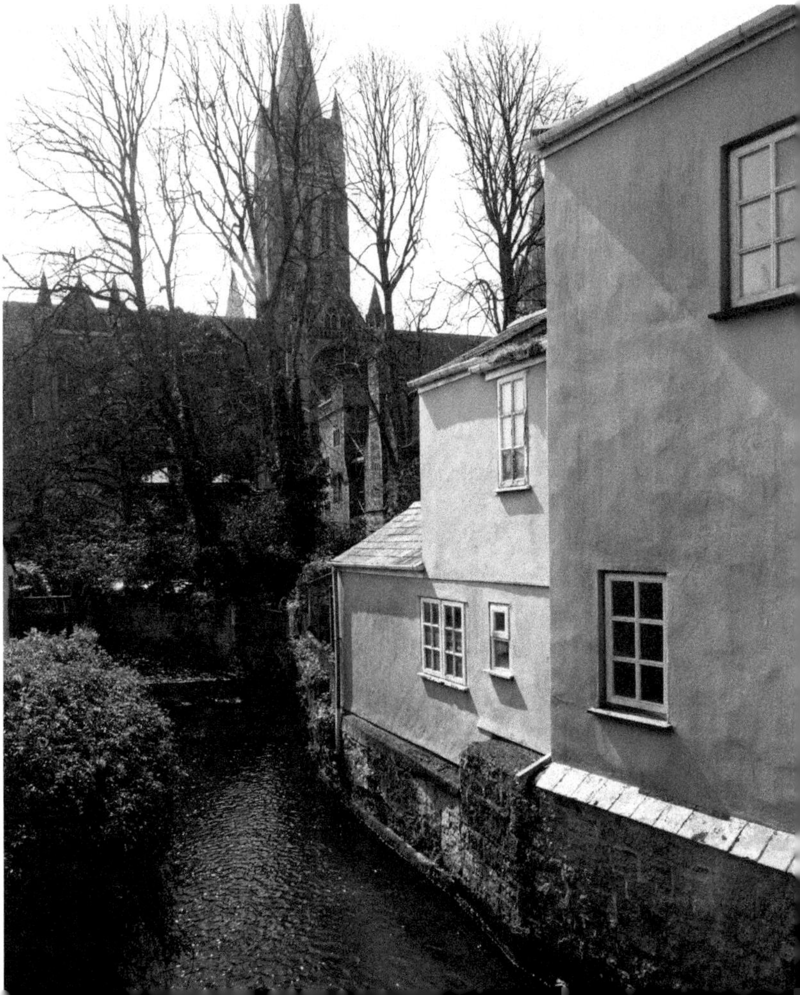

The River Allen runs through the city near Wilkes Walk.

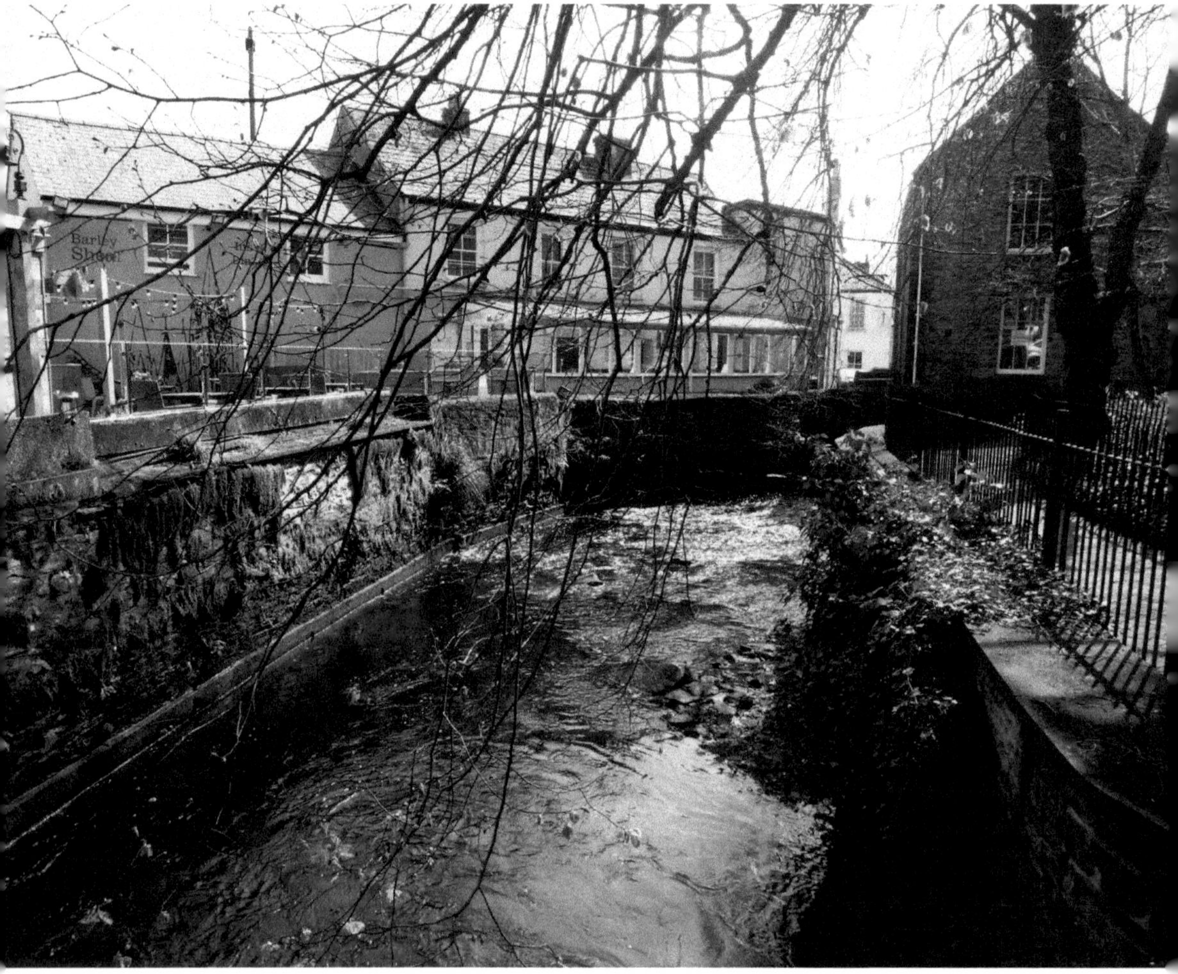

no more than a trickle. In a strange coincidence, there is also a footballer named River Allen who played as a mid-fielder for Truro City FC between 2017 and 2019.

Between the cathedral green and Wilkes Walk the river widens into what was once the millpool. Apart from powering the mill, the fast-flowing water was also used to power the blower of the Father Willis organ when the cathedral was first opened. It was also used as a bathing area for the elephants when the circus came to town!

Arms

After Queen Victoria granted Truro city status in 1877, a coat of arms was designed. It depicts a miner on the dexter (left-hand) side and a fisherman on the sinister (right-hand) side of a three-masted sailing ship at sea and two fish swimming beneath it. This reflects the industries most associated with Cornwall and which gave prosperity to the city. The motto *Exaltatum Cornu in Deo* was suggested by the city's first bishop, Bishop Benson, and translates as 'My horn is exalted in God', although horn in this context can be better translated as strength. An Old Testament quotation based on Hannah's song in the first Book of Samuel, it is used here as a play on words using the common derivations of the Latin word for horn (*cornu*) and the name Cornwall, which is itself horn-shaped. The arms are displayed on a number of buildings in the city, ranging from the Passmore Edwards Library building in Pydar Street to an ornate public convenience dating from 1925 in Lower Lemon Street.

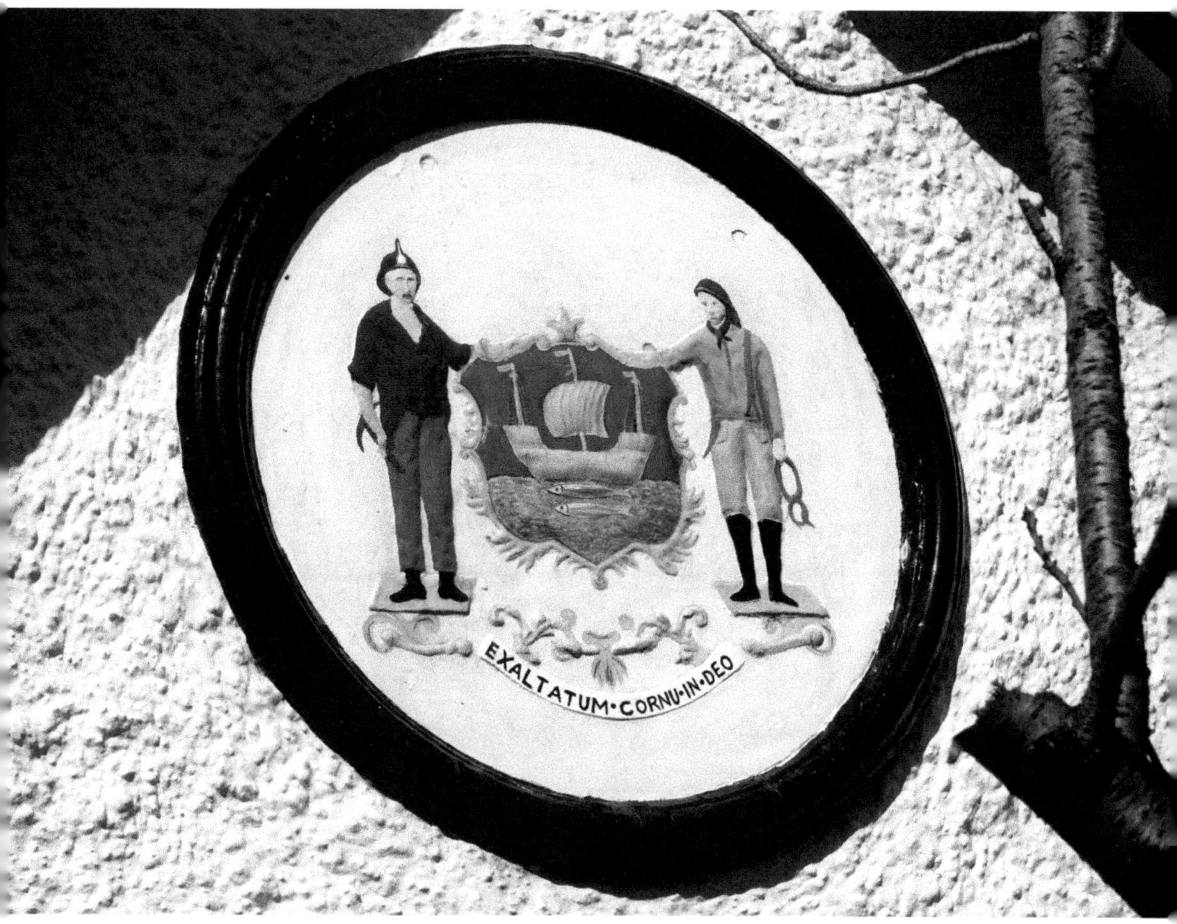

Truro's coat of arms on the public convenience in Lower Lemon Street, dating from 1925.

B

Bone, Henry

Henry Bone was born in Truro in 1755. His father was a woodcarver and cabinetmaker, and clearly, Henry inherited his craftsmanship, although it was applied to very different materials. At the age of sixteen, now living in Plymouth, Henry was apprenticed to William Cookworthy, discoverer of Cornish china clay and pioneer of porcelain manufacture, who had set up a porcelain works in the city. In 1772, when Cookworthy moved his factory to Bristol, Bone moved with him and spent six years as a painter of fine china. After the factory closed, Bone moved to London and began working for the city's watchmakers as an enameller. Soon he started painting miniatures onto ivory, and later onto enamel, and his study of his new wife Elizabeth was exhibited at the Royal Academy in 1780. His reputation steadily grew, and in 1797 he was appointed as enamel painter to the Prince of Wales. In due course, similar appointments followed to George III, William IV and George IV. In 1811 he was elected to the Royal Academy, and shortly afterwards painted one of the largest enamels ever seen, a copy of *Bacchus and Ariadne* by Titian. He sold this for the astonishing sum of 2,200 guineas, managing to cash the cheque a few hours before the bank folded. It sold at Christies in 2013 for £313,000. He retired in 1831 due to failing sight, and died in 1834. His eldest son, Henry, also became a successful enamel painter, as did two of his grandsons.

'Old Dreadnought' Boscawen

Edward Boscawen was the third son of Hugh Boscawen, the first Lord Falmouth. He was born in 1711 at the family seat of Tregothnan, downriver from Truro on the Roseland bank of the Fal. He had a dual career, a stellar one in the Royal Navy, and a second as the MP for Truro beginning in 1742, the same year as he married. His parliamentary career must have taken a back seat as his life was spent sailing from action to action, beginning with the War of Jenkin's Ear, the Austrian Succession, and ending with the Seven Years' War, subsequently living at Hatchland's Park in Surrey until his death in 1761, at the age of only fifty.

The young Edward entered the navy at the age of twelve, serving under Admiral Francis Hosier in the West Indies. He earned his nickname during the Seven Years' War as commander of HMS *Dreadnought*, when he captured the French ship *Médée* taking 800 prisoners. He was promoted to Admiral in 1758 and defeated the French fleet the year after. This earned him a lucrative position as commander of the marines and a seat on the Privy Council. He is buried in the Boscawen family vault at the church of St Michael Penkevil at Tregothnan. His name is commemorated in Boscawen Street and Boscawen Park.

Bosvigo Gardens

On the edge of the city by the Kenwyn valley, Bosvigo is hidden away up a drive beside a modern suburban estate, and describes itself as Cornwall's best-kept secret. The house is thought to date back to medieval times, although nothing that old remains today. It was replaced in the seventeenth century with a two-storey house built using cob, which now forms the centre portion of the present house. In the early eighteenth century it was one of several properties owned by mining magnate William Lemon. Two wings were added in 1780 and in the nineteenth century the house was enlarged

Bosvigo: the house and the conservatory.

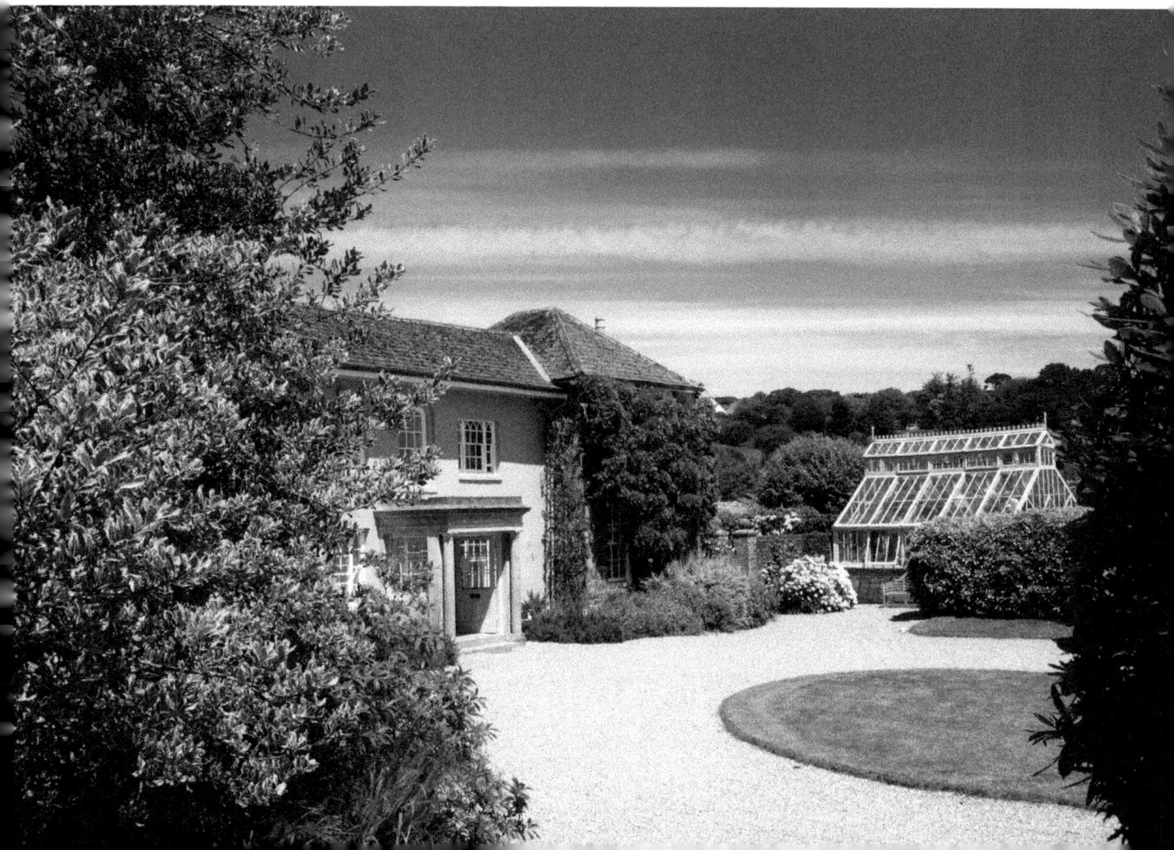

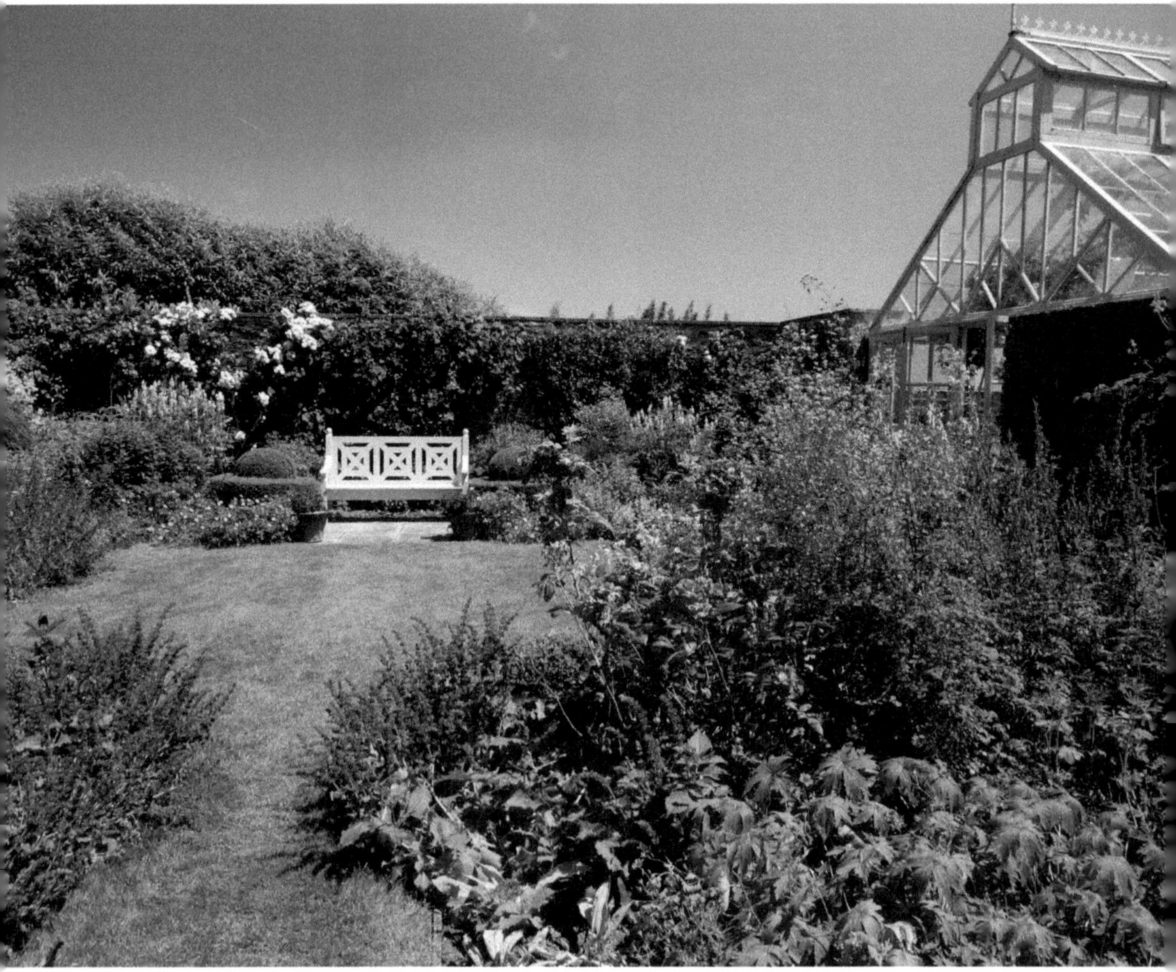

with the addition of a further wing, which the current owner, Wendy Perry, has now had demolished to restore a more balanced appearance to the house.

The gardens are set among trees and have been designed to be at their best during the summer months, providing some variety for horticulturalists in a county dominated by spring gardens. There is a walled garden adjoining the house where the Victorian wing once stood: the walls were built using the stones from its demolition and the impressive Victorian conservatory now stands on its own as a summerhouse. The garden is planted with pink- and blue-flowering species such as old-fashioned roses, campanulas and asters. The hot garden across the driveway is planted with red- and orange-flowering dahlias and salvias all chosen to explode into a firework display of colour during August. There is also a geometrically laid out Vean garden and a woodland walk. The garden is open for three days a week during summer and the website gives details.

C

Calenick

This quiet little hamlet lies at the end of Calenick Creek to the west of Newham, just off the Newham Trail. You wouldn't think it today, but in the eighteenth and nineteenth centuries this peaceful backwater was a noisy and smoke-ridden hub of the tin smelting industry. In 1702 a new method of smelting tin ore was invented, which used cheap sea coal in place of expensive charcoal. The new furnaces using the process were sited at Newham close to the quay where coal could be brought in from Wales. In 1711 they were moved upriver to Calenick where there was a fast-flowing stream, the aptly named River Tinney. The works became part of the empire belonging to William Lemon and after his death in 1760 it was purchased by his former clerk Thomas 'Guinea a Minute' Daniell (see separate entry). The smelting works continued in operation until 1891, by which time ownership had passed to the Daubuz family. The fine slate-hung Queen Anne-style mansion with its separate clock tower (built in 1752), which can be seen from the road today, was actually the account

The old smelting office at Calenick with its clock tower.

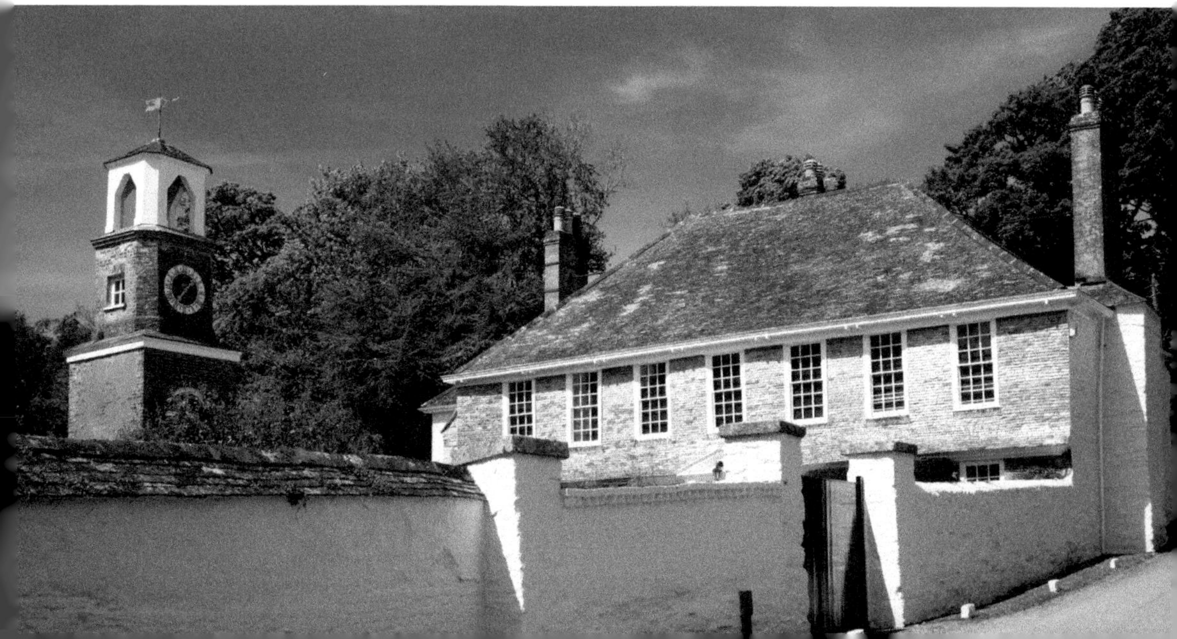

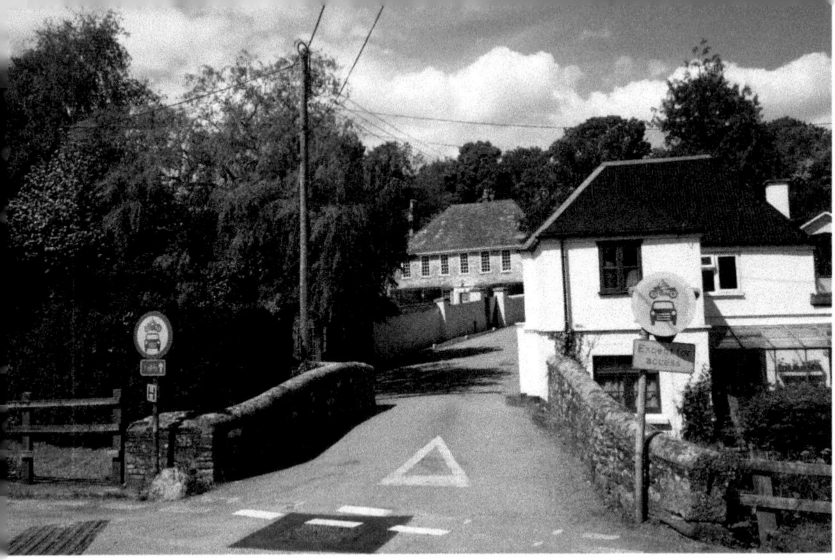

Left: Calenick village.

Below: Workers' cottages, Calenick.

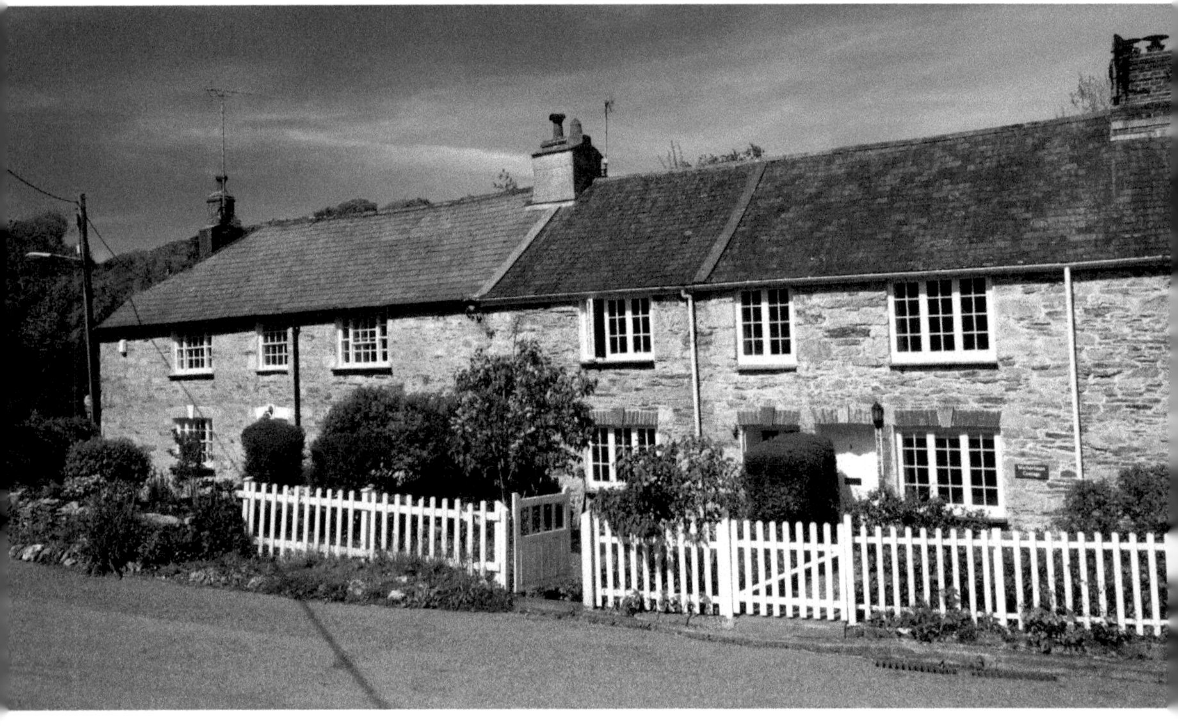

offices for the smelting works. The bell in the clock tower is inscribed with William Lemon's name. Eventually the creek became silted up with an estimated 10,000 tons of waste from tin mines further upstream.

Born here in 1807 was Nicholas Michell, the son of John Michell, who worked as a chemist in the smelting industry and was known as the father of the tin trade. One of their ancestors, Peter, sailed around the world with Sir Francis Drake. Nicholas attended Truro Grammar School and worked in the smelting works as a young man, later moving to London where he became a popular poet after publishing *The Ruins of Many Lands* in 1849.

Cathedral of the Blessed Virgin Mary

In 1876 an Act of Parliament separated Cornwall from the Diocese of Exeter and created the Diocese of Truro, covering nearly 1,400 square miles. On 28 August 1877 a royal proclamation was issued which created the City of Truro, and a new cathedral was planned which was to be built on the site of the existing parish church of St Mary the Virgin. The architect was John Loughborough Pearson, who preserved the south aisle of the church and incorporated it into his design. The church originally dated from the twelfth century and had been rebuilt in the sixteenth. A tall and elegant spire was added in 1769, creating a very un-Cornish church building. The demolition of the north aisle and tower in 1880 meant the loss of the spire, the top portion of which was preserved and kept in the grounds of the Diocesan offices at Kenwyn. When the offices closed in 2015, the spire was re-sited in the cathedral grounds. In order to make space for the cathedral a number of buildings in the centre of the town were purchased and demolished, but even so the space was very limited, resulting in the choir and nave being deliberately misaligned.

In 1889 William Gladstone, at the time between premierships, visited Truro and had a look at progress, pronouncing that he was delighted with the building so far. By then, though, building work had ceased temporarily while more funds were raised. Pearson died in 1897 before its completion, and when work was restarted in 1898, Pearson's son Frank took charge until the cathedral was finished in 1910. The central spire is dedicated to Queen Victoria, and the two western spires, slightly smaller, to Edward VII and Queen Alexandria. There was not enough money to roof them in copper, like the smaller bell-tower, or for the medieval-style cloisters Pearson had planned; a modern chapter house was added in the 1960s. Local stone was used as much as possible, with Cornish granite from Mabe and St Stephens featuring prominently. Bath stone was used for the decorative work, which on the exterior has been found to erode quite quickly in the salt air of Cornwall. Recent restoration work has replaced this with Cotswold stone, of similar appearance but more resistant to weathering.

On 8 July 1908 a serious accident took place, the only one occurring during the building work. A steam lift had been raised to the top of one of the western towers to take

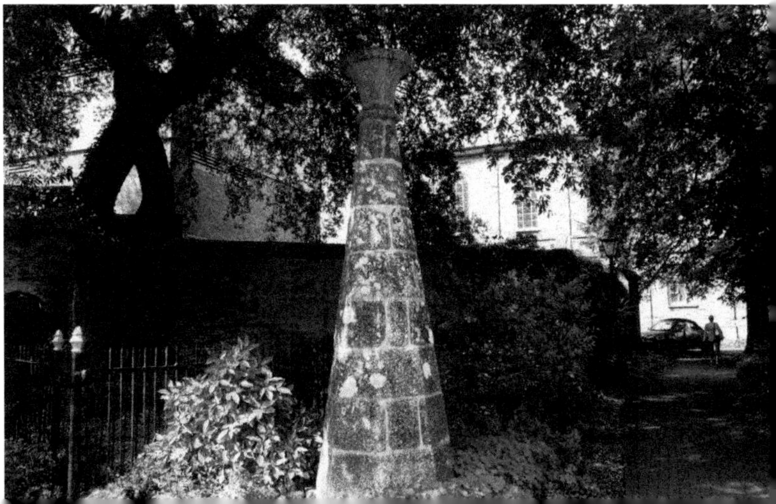

The spire from St Mary's Church, in the grounds of Truro Cathedral.

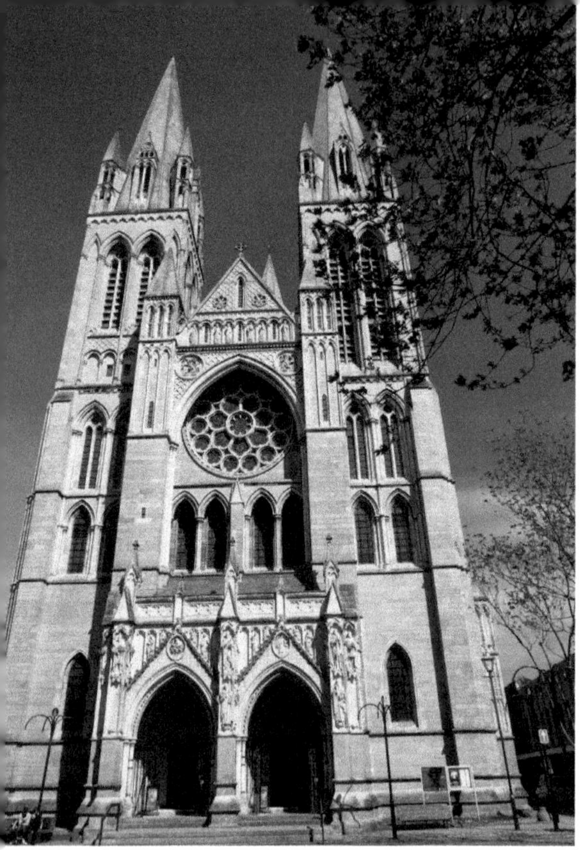
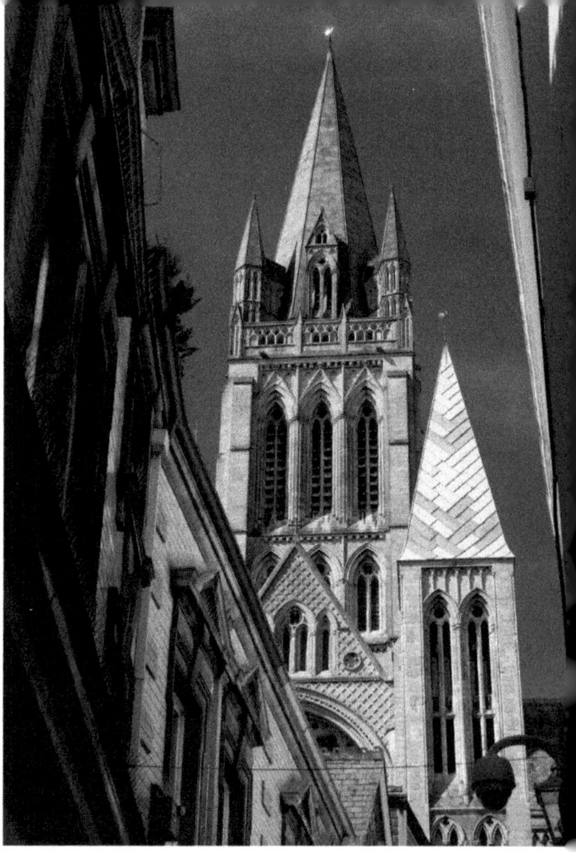

Above: Cathedral west front (*left*), and Victoria tower and St Mary's camponile (*right*).

Below: Detail from exterior carvings by Nathaniel Hitch: Truro Cathedral architect J. L. Pearson (*left*) and (*right*) Bishop E. W. Benson.

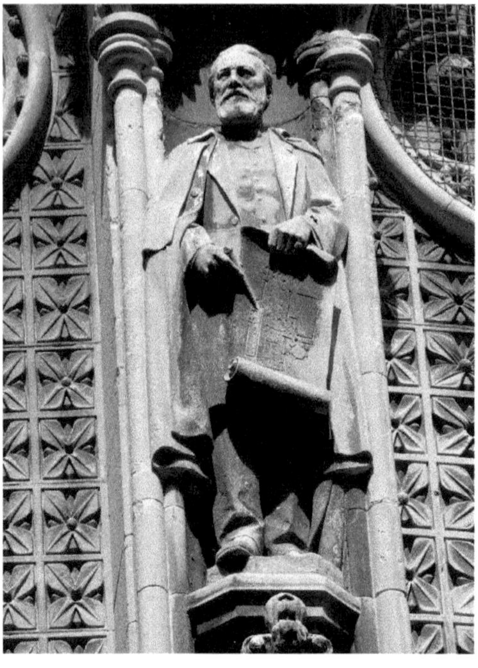
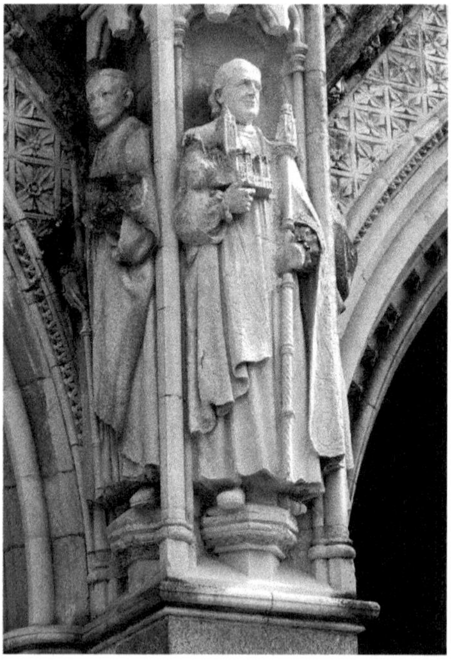

materials up to the construction workers. It was 1 p. m. and after the materials had been unloaded, six workmen coming off their morning shift stepped into the cage to return to the ground. Reports suggest that the safety device had not been applied correctly, and the driver was unaware of their actions and had not applied steam pressure to control the descent. Consequently, the weight of the men caused the cage to plummet 70 feet to the ground with six men inside. Five escaped with less severe injuries, but fifty-one-year-old Richard Granville sustained injuries to both legs, which had to be amputated. He was given artificial limbs but was unable to work again and received £300 in compensation. He also received assistance, and also achieved a degree of fame, from local business Furniss & Co. (see Furniss, John Cooper), and lived for another twenty-five years.

Inside, Pearson wanted to create a space that would 'bring people soonest to their knees'. The reredos, in Bath stone, is by Nathaniel Hitch, who also carved the exterior. It depicts Christ crucified and above, glorified in Heaven. Of the smaller items, a glorious oil painting by John Miller, *Cornubria: Land of the Saints*, depicts Cornwall seen from space with its churches depicted as Celtic crosses and the cathedral bathed in a shaft of light from Heaven. It was commissioned for the centenary of the laying of the foundation stone in 1980. There are more everyday works of art on display too, such as the matchstick model of the cathedral made by Bill Cheshire using more than 40,000 matches, taking him 1,600 hours of work. The cathedral's stained-glass windows are among the finest Victorian glass in the country. The east lancet windows above the

Model of Truro Cathedral made from matchsticks, by Bill Cheshire.

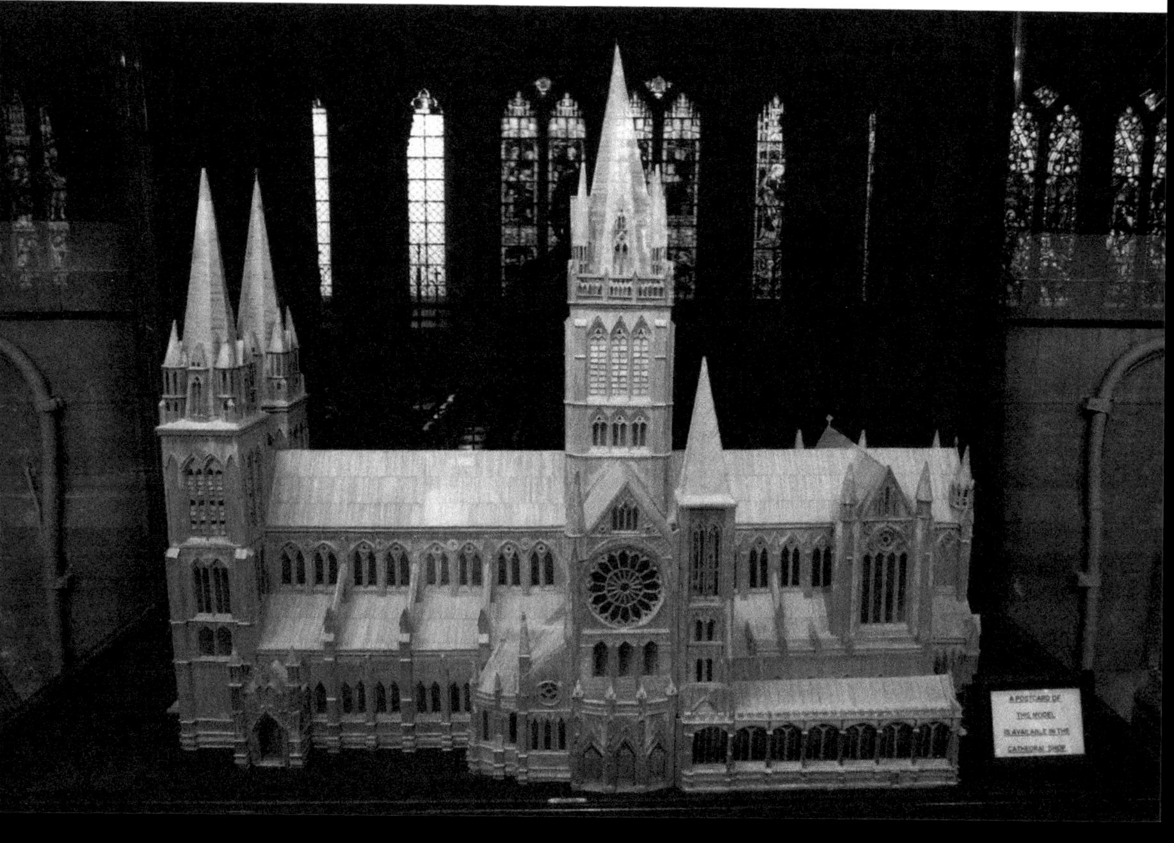

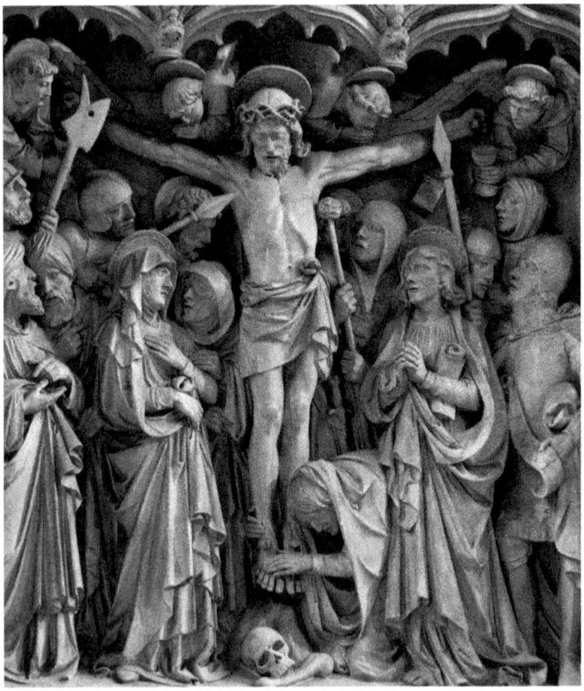

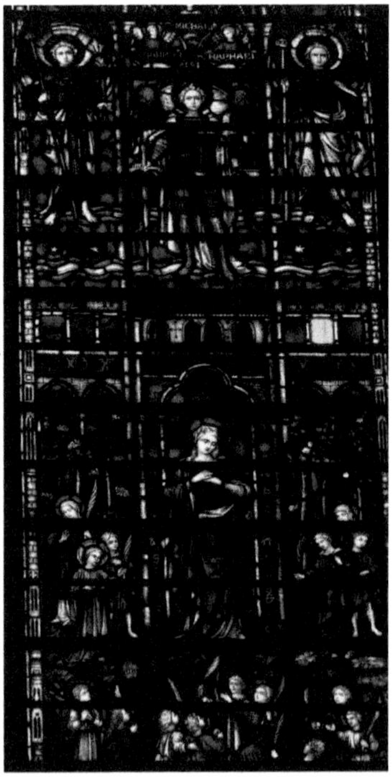

Reredos by Nathaniel Hitch (*left*) and (*right*) east lancet windows showing accidental damage.

high altar are worth examining more closely as they sustained damage during the Second World War – not from enemy bombs however, but from an errant choirboy who managed to shoot out one of the panes with an air rifle! The blue glass needed for the repair was difficult to obtain in wartime, and the story goes that someone found a piece of blue glass in an old door and this was used to make a temporary repair, one which is still in place! The much lighter shade of blue can clearly be seen from the quire. As a postscript, some twenty years ago the transgressor, without his gun, returned to the cathedral for a service and introduced himself to the bishop.

Catholic Church of Our Lady of the Portal and St Piran

This modern church replaced a smaller late Victorian building in Chapel Hill, designed by the prolific Silvanus Trevail (see separate entry). Dating from 1973, all we see from the street is a simple undecorated concrete block, but this is surely a church that demands a look at the interior. Its unusual aspect ratio creates an extremely wide space, rather like a theatre, bringing the congregation much closer to the celebrant. The walls are decorated with the stations of the cross and stained glass, by Fr Charles Norris of Buckfast Abbey, is sparingly used above the altar, directing light downwards. The altar is framed by two

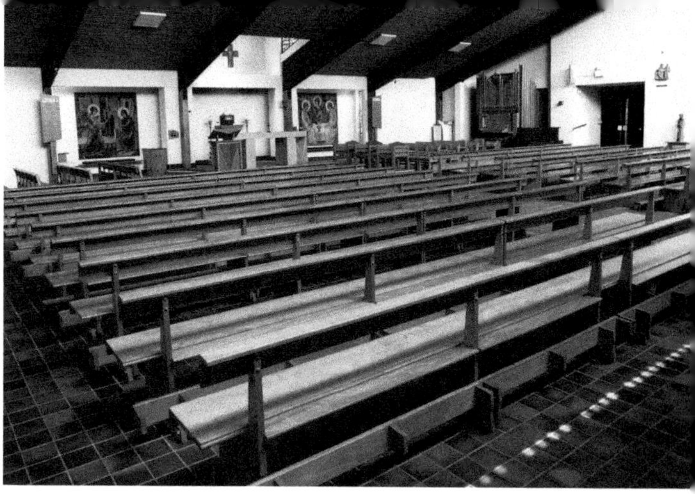

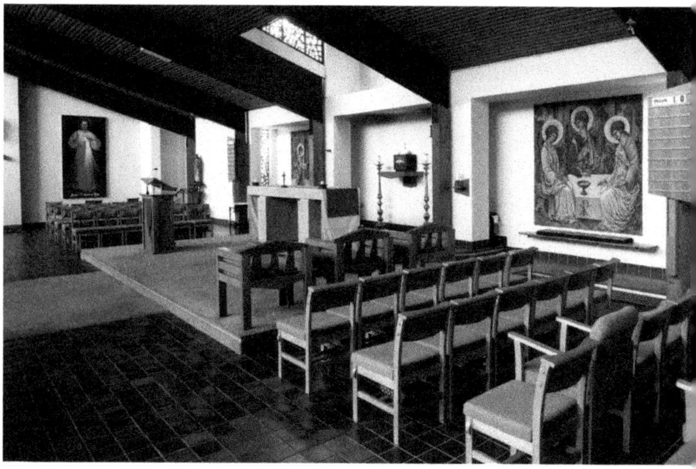

Interior, of the Catholic Church of St Piran and Our Lady of the Portal.

paintings, the work of a former parishioner, and based on fifteenth-century Russian icons by Rublev. The unusual dedication to Our Lady of the Portal goes back to a medieval chapel, long gone, on this western side of Truro whose role was to maintain a bridging point over the river. This is the only church in England with this dedication. Another unique feature is a spring-fed well discovered during the building of the church. It is inside the church, covered by a slate slab and inscribed *Fons Mariae matris pastoris et agni*, which translates as 'the well of Mary, mother of the Shepherd and Lamb'.

A much-loved former priest was Irishman Fr Norbert Jones, incumbent during the last decade of the nineteenth century, who loved to chat to everyone he met on his way around the city: he spent so much time walking the streets that he became known as Tramping Truro Jones.

City of Lights Festival

Brightening up the darkness (literally) in November, Truro's annual parade of paper lanterns has been a winter attraction since 1996. Schools and businesses take part with the help of professional artists by constructing huge sculptures made from withy and

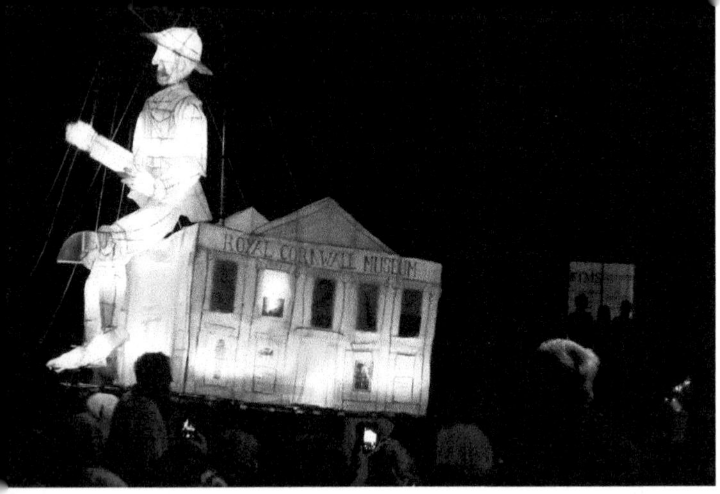

Left and below: City of Lights parade in Lemon Street.

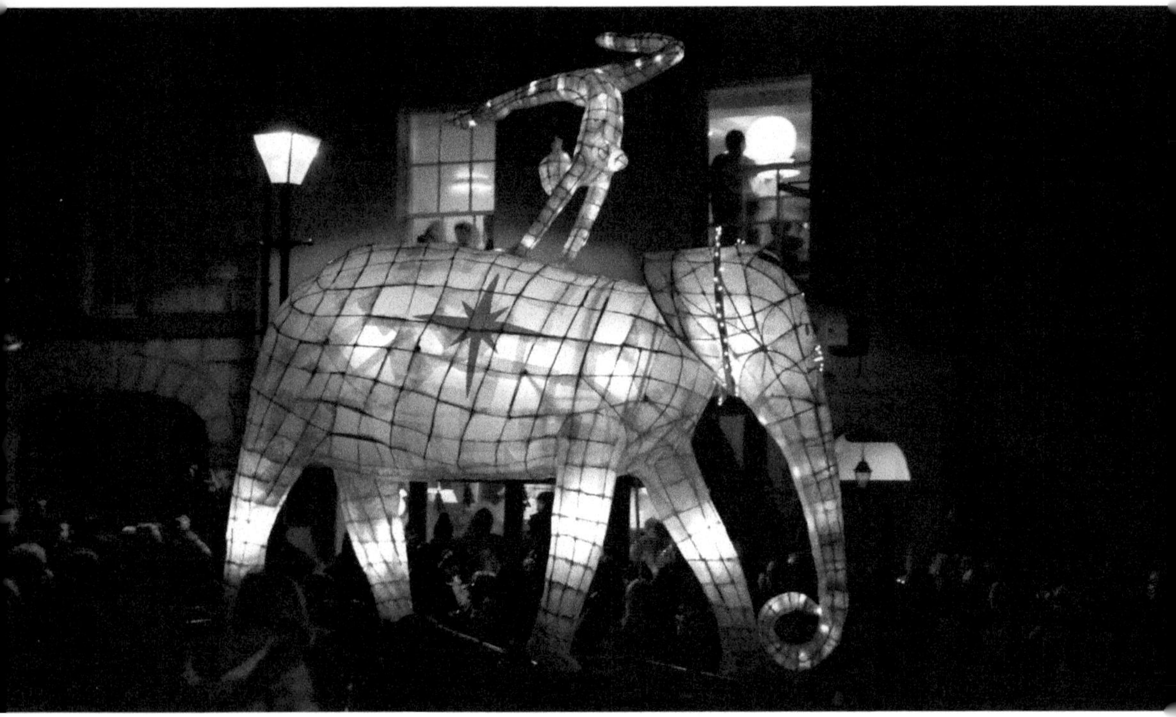

tissue. Some walking, others carried on the back of trucks, the parade is accompanied by music and dancing, and follows a route around the city streets. Each year has a different theme and the parade also visits nearby towns and villages during November.

Compton Castle

Built in 1914 by Cox & Co. in Falmouth, the paddle steamer *Compton Castle* was one of three such vessels used for passenger excursions between Totnes and Dartmouth on the River Dart. Apart from an interruption during the Second World War when she was requisitioned as a munitions carrier, *Compton Castle* plied her trade on the

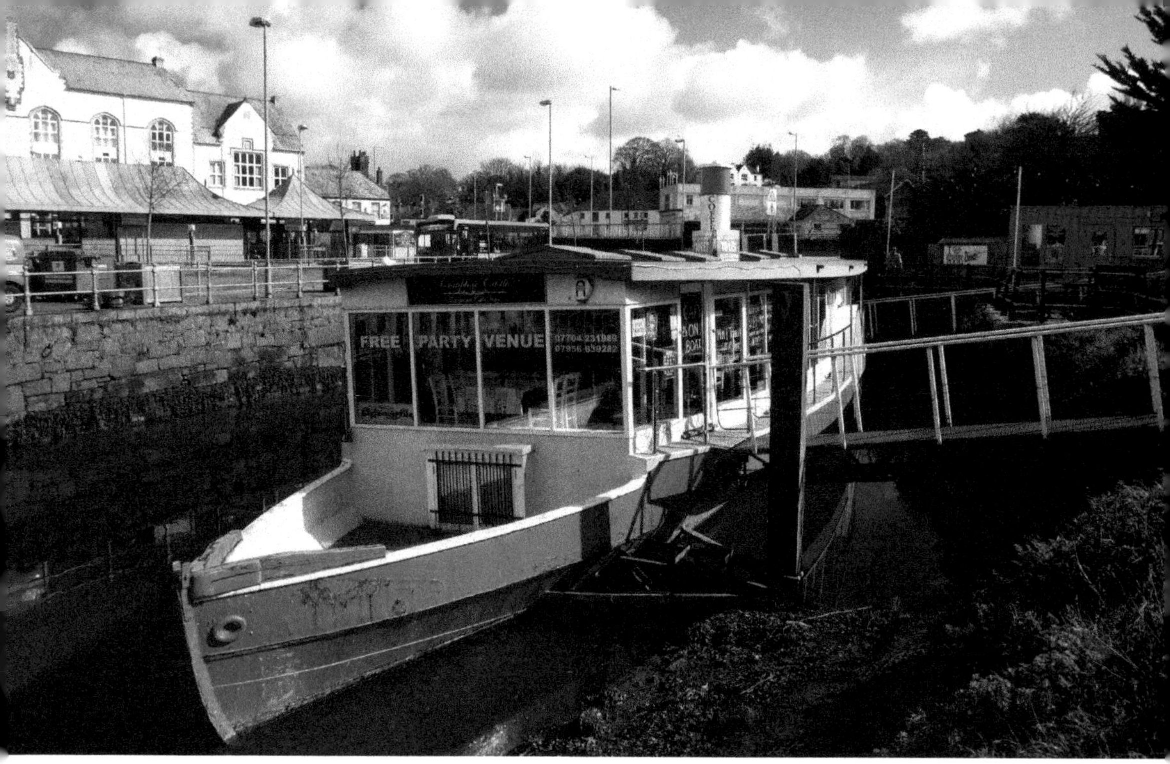

PS *Compton Castle* moored at Lemon Quay.

Dart until she was withdrawn from service in 1962. She then spent several years as a floating café at Ivybridge before moving to Looe where it was hoped she might be restored to her former glory. When it became clear that restoration was not feasible, her engines were removed and in 1982 she arrived at a mud berth on Lemon Quay and was used as a floating florist's shop and, until recently, a café. At the time of writing she is available to lease. The engines were purchased by the owners of her sister ship, the *Kingswear Castle*, which is still in service on the River Dart. She is not the first River Dart steamer on the Truro River; between 1841 and 1843 the paddle steamer *Dart* plied between Falmouth and Truro.

Community of the Epiphany

This Anglican order was founded in 1883 by Bishop George Wilkinson, second Bishop of Truro, along with Miss Julian Warrender, who later became Sister Superior. Assisting with the running of the cathedral, the sisters also founded daughter houses around Cornwall, and ran a school in Truro and a convalescent home in St Agnes. In 1936 their influence even extended to Japan, where they founded the Community of Nazareth in Tokyo.

The community was based at Alverton Manor, a large early nineteenth-century house on the eastern side of the city which was put up for sale by the Tweedy family in 1881. The house was extended by the addition of a bell tower and accommodation wing, and in 1908 a magnificent chapel designed by architect G. H. Seddon was completed.

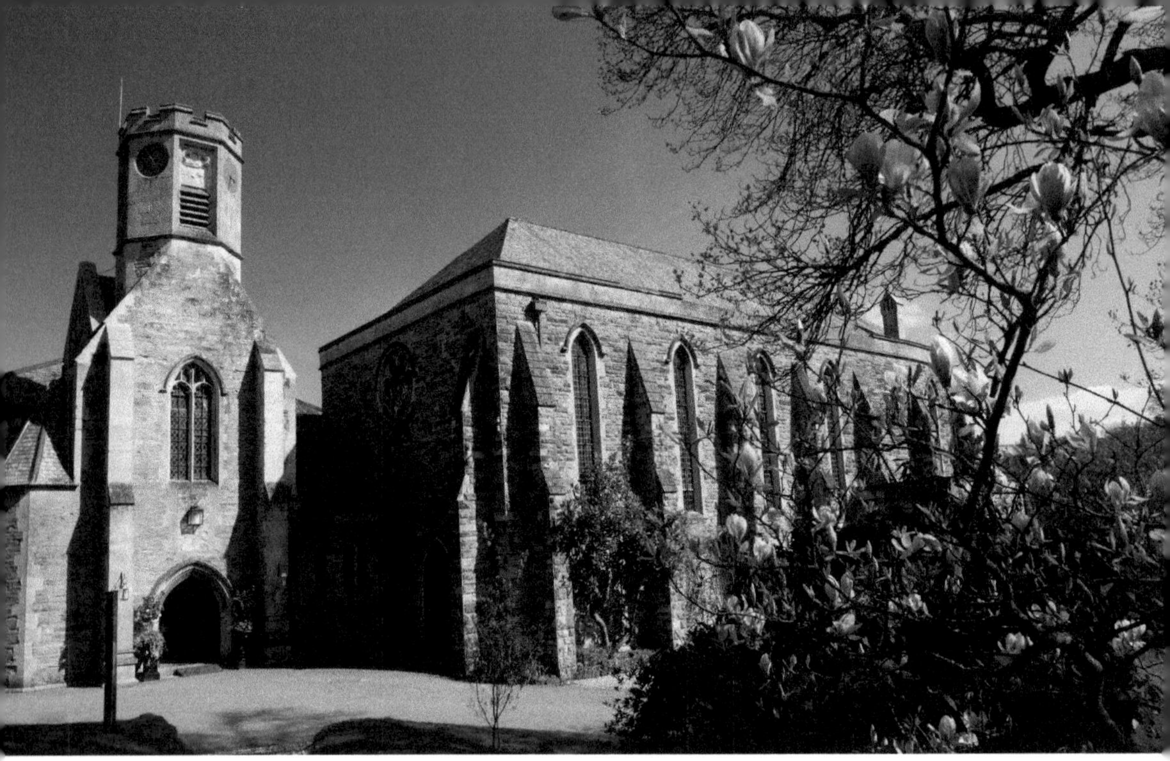

Alverton Manor (now The Alverton), former home of the Community of the Epiphany.

In 1904 Florence Maybrick, an American who had spent fifteen years in prison for allegedly murdering her husband (thought by some to have been Jack the Ripper) by administering arsenic, was released from Aylesbury prison and served the last six months of her sentence at the convent in order to ease her return to normal life. This was arranged by the Duchess of Bedford, a noted philanthropist of the day. At the convent Maybrick's true identity was kept secret from all but the Sister Superior and the local police constable, and her cover story was that she was recovering from a bout of influenza. Maybrick described her time at the convent, which she spent sewing and going on long walks in the grounds, as the most peaceful and happiest of her entire life.

The community continued at Alverton until 1984, when, with their numbers in decline, the twelve remaining sisters moved to the former bishop's palace and former home of the Cathedral School, then named Copeland Court, in Kenwyn. Alverton Manor was sold and is now a hotel, with the chapel used as a wedding and conference venue. The last remaining sisters left in 2001 and Sister Elizabeth, the last survivor, died at the age of 101 in 2017. The name of the order lives on at Copeland Court, which was renamed Epiphany House and which is now run as a retreat and conference centre (see also Sister Emilie).

Courts of Justice

Cornwall's county court moved from Bodmin to Truro in 1988. The Grade II listed court building, which cost £3.5 million, was designed by Eldred Evans and David

Shalev, who also designed the Tate Gallery building in St Ives, built a few years later and which shares the same rotunda style. The court building won the RIBA Building of the Year Award, and the editor of the *Architect's Journal* described it as an extremely civilised building in which the administration of justice can take place. It is designed in the post-modernist style with a pedimented entrance portico, and the three courts are arranged around a naturally lit atrium. Backing onto Victoria Gardens, the new court stands on the site of the medieval castle. Until 1983 the site was the home of the cattle market, now moved to new premises on the western side of the city.

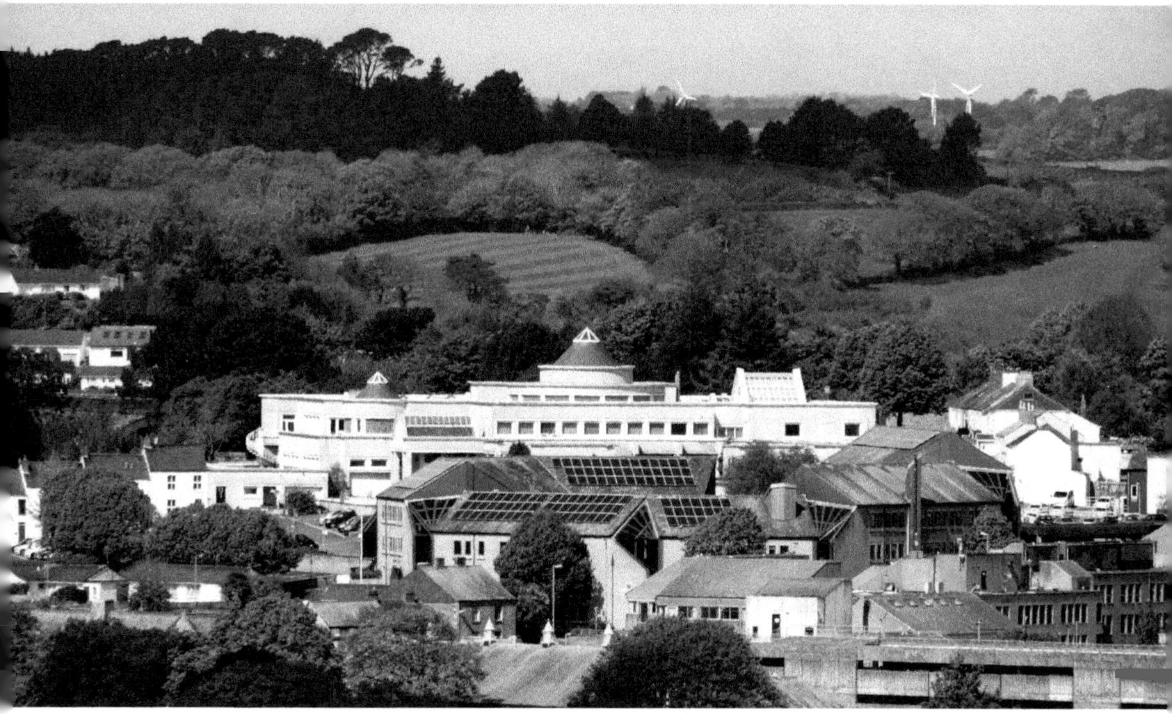

Above and right: Truro's Courts of Justice, built in 1988 on the site of the castle.

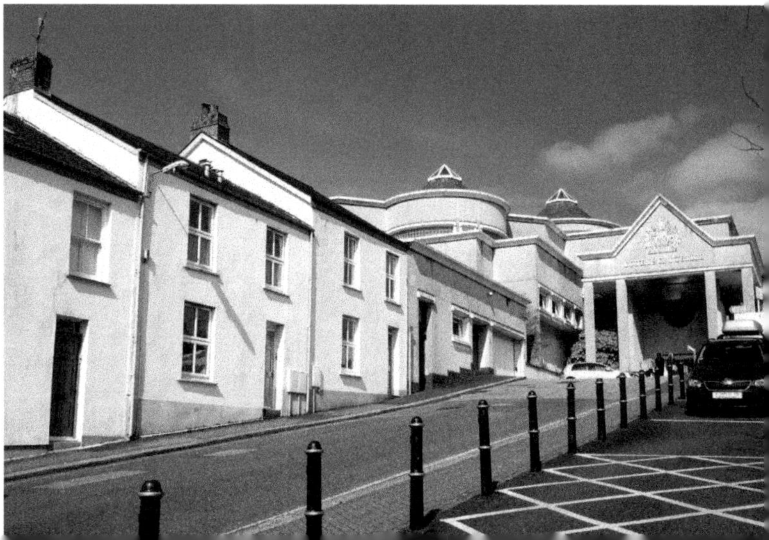

D

Daubuz Moor

The area known as Daubuz Moor is a 14-acre site which has been given to the city as a nature reserve. Formerly water meadows bordering the River Allen, it lies just off Moresk Road beyond the railway viaduct at the eastern end of the city. It was donated by Revd Charles Reginald Saltren Enys, from the estate of the same name near

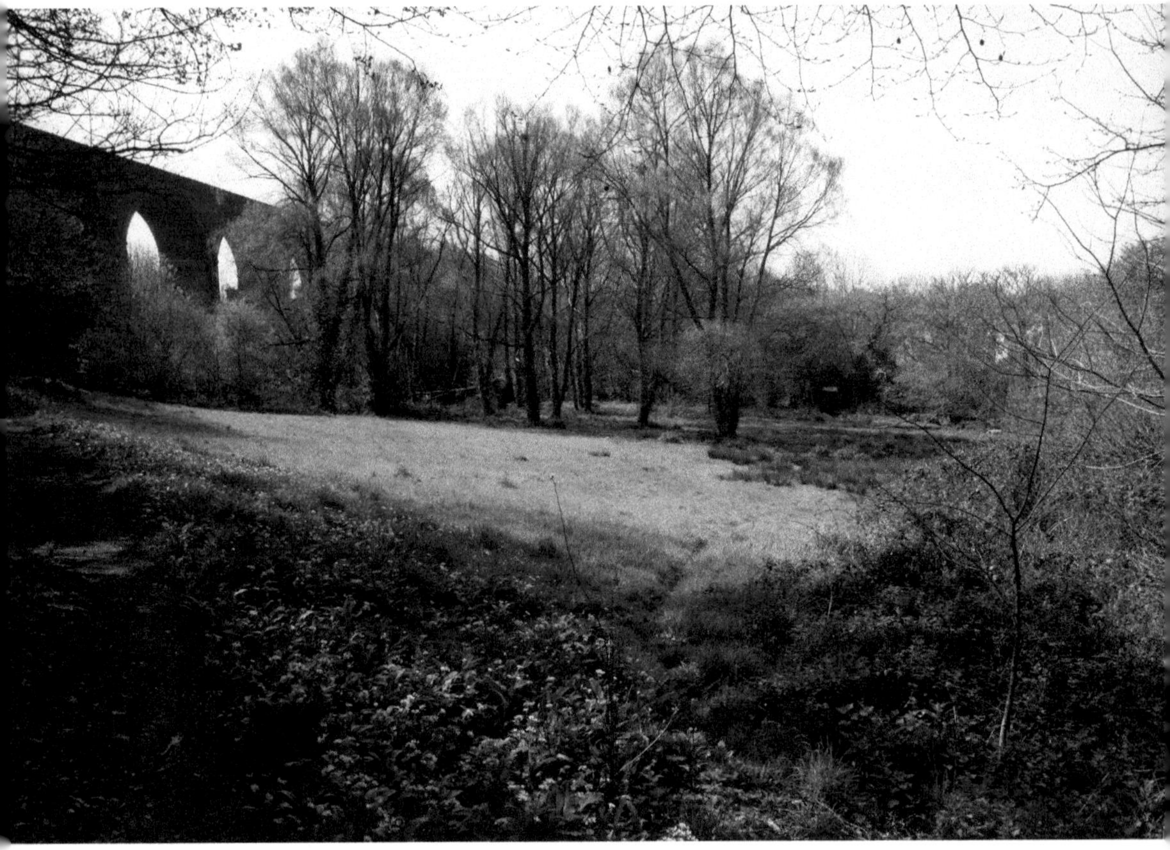

Daubuz Moor is a nature reserve on the edge of the city.

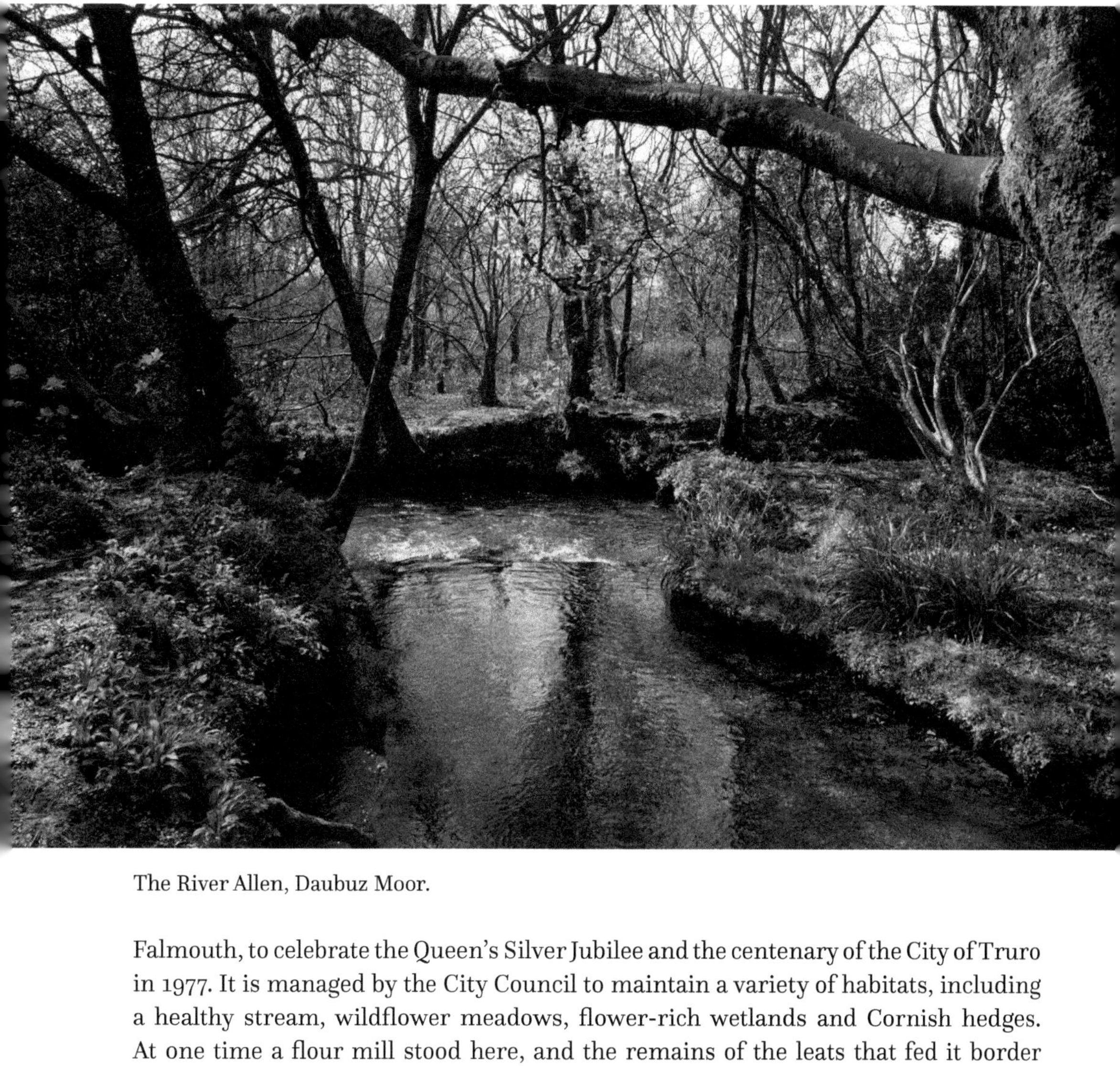

The River Allen, Daubuz Moor.

Falmouth, to celebrate the Queen's Silver Jubilee and the centenary of the City of Truro in 1977. It is managed by the City Council to maintain a variety of habitats, including a healthy stream, wildflower meadows, flower-rich wetlands and Cornish hedges. At one time a flour mill stood here, and the remains of the leats that fed it border the footpath. The area is named after Lewis Daubuz (1755–1839), an industrialist of French extraction who had made his money from tin smelting at Carvedras and who planted gardens in the vicinity.

Drummer Statue

Standing outside the Hall for Cornwall on Lemon Quay is a 15-foot-high bronze statue of a naked drummer. It is the work of sculptor Tim Shaw, who cast the dynamic figure partly from copper and tin mined in Cornwall. The statue was created in a disused granite quarry in the county, the stone from which had paved London's streets, and embodies its creator's belief that Cornwall is a place where the drum beats differently. It was unveiled in June 2011 by another famous drummer, Roger Taylor from the band Queen (see separate entry), who grew up in Truro. The figure, which cost £95,000, has provoked a mixed reaction among Truronians, some outraged at the anatomical detail, others hailing the sculpture as a great addition to the city's cultural heritage.

In 2018, prior to the refurbishment of the Hall for Cornwall, the statue was temporarily removed and at the time of writing is on show at the Eden Project near St Austell. It will return to Truro in 2020.

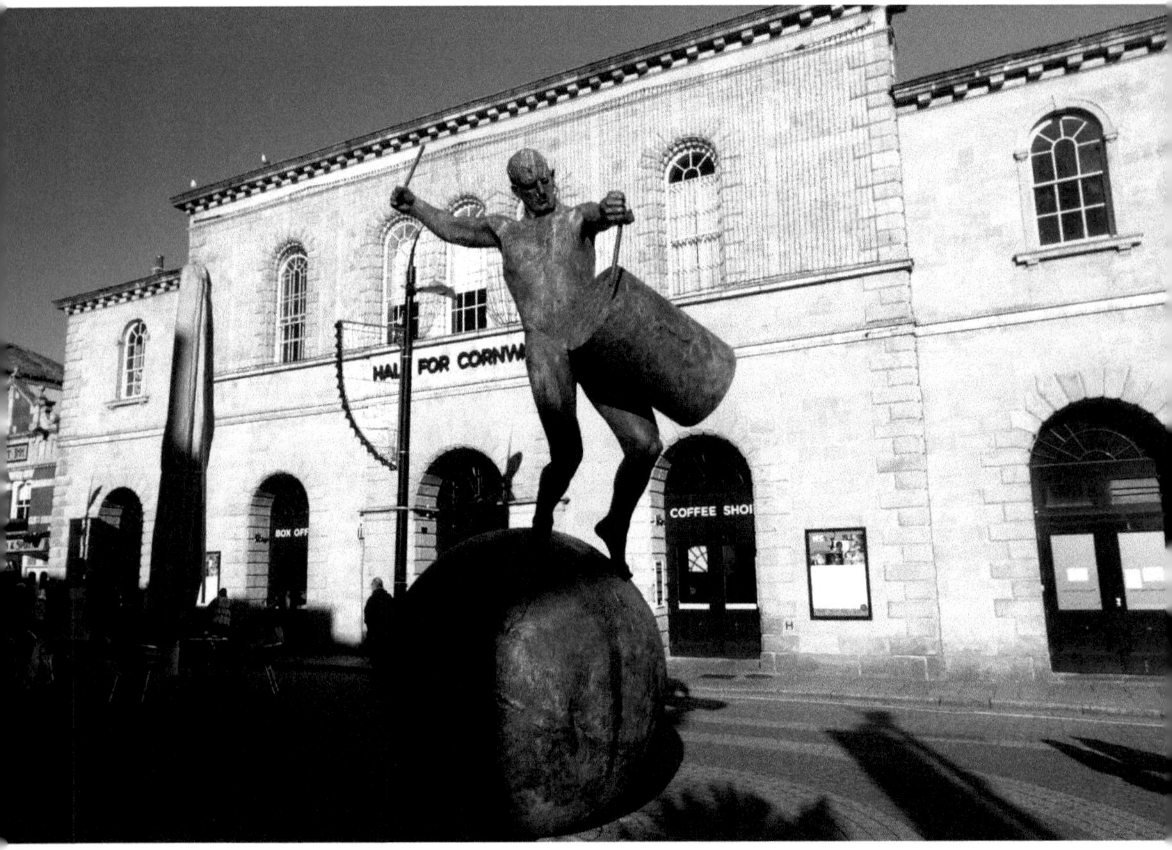

Tim Shaw's Drummer statue stands outside the Hall for Cornwall.

Emidy, Joseph

When Joseph Antonio Emidy died in Truro in 1835, he was one of the most celebrated virtuoso musicians in Cornwall. He played the violin, was leader of the Truro Philharmonic Orchestra, and taught throughout the county. He was also a composer, writing chamber music, concertos and symphonies. Joseph was born in Guinea, West Africa, in 1775, and at the age of twelve was captured by Portuguese slave traders. After being taken to Brazil, he ended up in Portugal, where his musical talents were much appreciated and he played in the orchestra of Lisbon Opera House.

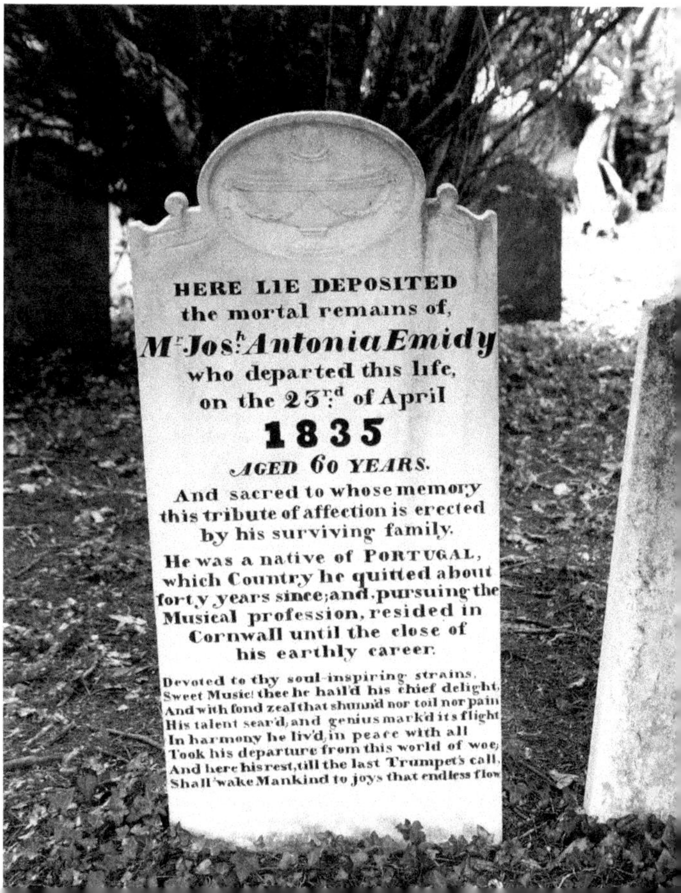

The grave of Joseph Emidy in Kenwyn churchyard.

In 1795, during the Napoleonic Wars, his fortunes took a turn for the worse when naval captain Sir Edward Pellew, from a Cornish naval family and who had attended Truro Grammar School, heard his playing and ordered his kidnapping to replace a missing ship's fiddler. Joseph spent four miserable years at sea on HMS *Indefatigable* before being discharged in Falmouth in 1799. In 1802 he married Jenefer Hutchins and built his musical career for a second time, moving to Truro in 1815. He is reported to have been an exquisite violinist, and was also able to teach the 'cello, flute, clarinet, Spanish guitar and piano. He became the best-known composer in south-west England and his music was introduced to London by the anti-slavery campaigner James Silk Buckingham, who Emidy had taught to play the flute and who had dubbed him the Cornish Mendelssohn. Joseph never made it to the capital as it was feared that 'his colour would go against him'. Sadly, none of the scores of his musical compositions have survived. He had eight children, and following his death in 1835, he was buried in the churchyard at Kenwyn. His story has been imaginatively told in the book *The Boy Who Played His Way to Freedom* by Bernadette Jameson, who is married to one of his descendants.

In September 2007, the year marking the 200th anniversary of the abolition of slavery in Britain, a special service was held in Kenwyn church to mark the restoration of his gravestone. The work was paid for by the Emidy Trust, an organisation set up to foster cultural links between Cornwall and West Africa. His inscription reads:

> Here we deposited the mortal remains
> Of Mr JOS ANTONIO EMIDY
> Who departed this life on 23rd April 1835 aged 60 years
> And sacred to whose memory this tribute of affection is erected by his surviving family.
> He was a native of Portugal which country he quitted about forty years since, and pursuing the musical profession, resided in Cornwall until the close of his earthly career.
>
> Devoted to thy soul inspiring strains, Sweet Music! Thee he hailed his chief delight
> And with fond zeal that shunned nor toil nor pain
> His talent seared and genius marked his flight.
> In harmony he lived, in peace with all
> Took his departure from this world of woe
> And here his rest 'til the last trumpet call
> Shall wake mankind to joy that endless flows.

Sister Emilie

In 1889 Amelia Brice entered the Community of the Epiphany at Alverton House as a novice. On 7 May 1892 she took Holy Orders, taking the name of Sister Emilie. The same year she became head of Rosewin Training School for Servants, which the sisters ran in Truro.

In June 1908 Sister Emilie took a group of twenty teenaged girls from the school to spend two weeks on the Cornish coast at West Pentire. On the morning of 23 June, a group of girls were sitting on rocks overlooking the sea. They were well supervised and the sea conditions were not rough, but a sudden huge wave (which a witness compared to a tidal wave) washed the girls and their supervisor into the sea. The older girls swam to safety, but two of the youngest ones, Jane Searle and Annie Frost, were swept away. Sister Emilie, a non-swimmer, jumped into the water and made heroic attempts to save them, but lost consciousness after hitting her head on a rock, and was last seen floating face-down out to sea. The Crantock burial register records that a 'great wave' swept the girls from the rocks and they were drowned. Their bodies were recovered and buried in Crantock churchyard. Sister Emilie's body was not recovered until a fortnight later, when it was found by a fisherman still floating face-downwards several miles up the coast near Trevose Head. A note in the burial register records that it appeared unaffected by any trace of decomposition and her clothes were undamaged. She is buried in the churchyard at St Endellion and a memorial service was held in the cathedral, where a plaque to her memory was unveiled. For her part in trying to save Sister Emilie, Miss Isabel Miriams, who was learning Japanese at the convent before becoming a missionary, was later awarded the medal of the Royal Humane Society.

The grave of Sister Emilie in St Endellion churchyard.

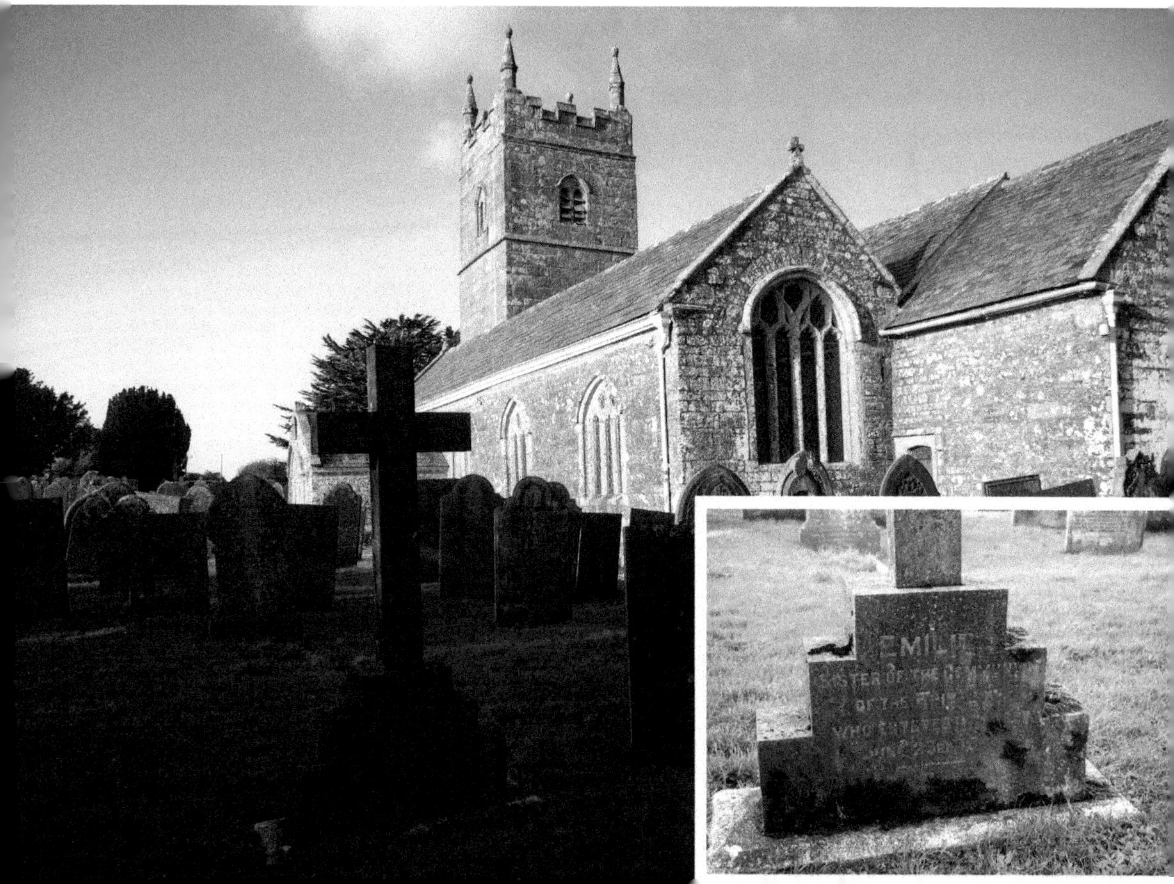

F

Foote, Samuel

Born in 1720, the son of a former magistrate of Truro, Samuel Foote was one of the most famous comedians and satirists of his day. He is associated with the Red Lion Hotel building in Boscawen Street, which was built by his relative John Foote in 1682, although it is uncertain whether Samuel ever lived there. He attended Truro Grammar School, where he showed a talent for mimicry: as a schoolboy he managed to fool his father by mimicking a family friend. Attracted by the theatrical side of the legal profession, he studied at Oxford where he was responsible for another prank after observing that the church at Worcester College had a bell rope which hung down in the porch. This adjoined a field upon which grazed a herd of cattle. He tied a bunch of hay to the end of the rope and, as he anticipated, in the middle of the night one of the cows tried to graze on the tempting morsel, ringing the bell and causing panic among the sleeping residents. After Oxford, he seemed to be destined for a career in court, starting at Temple Bar. However, he spent most of his time mingling with theatrical folk in the cafés of Covent Garden and started to live beyond his means, ending up with a brief spell in a debtor's prison by the age of twenty-two. He decided on an acting career as a means of increasing his income, and after failing to make much of an impression as Othello on the London stage, tried his hand in Ireland, where he was more successful. Returning to the London stage he joined the company of the Theatre Royal Drury Lane where he found his niche writing and performing in his own comedies, alongside David Garrick amongst others. He also engaged in a war of wit with another satirist, David Fielding. The success of this new type of political theatre led to censorship, for he had used previously written material without obtaining a licence. Constables descended on the theatre and removed the audience. Foote's legal brain found ways around this quite easily, instead inviting his audience to take chocolate or tea with him for a fee, during which he entertained them. He also made fun of his wife, who he referred to as a silly simpering girl, and when she suffered injuries falling out of a carriage, he compared her bruised face to a map of the world.

In 1766, whilst at a hunting party hosted by his sponsor Lord Mexborough and at which one of the guests was the Duke of York, Foote had an accident which was to change his fortunes. Boasting about his skill as a rider, he attempted to ride a particularly lively horse in order to create some amusement for the rest of the guests. Mexborough knew Foote was a poor rider, but did not anticipate what happened next: Foote was thrown off his steed and so badly injured his leg that it had to be amputated there and then. In recompense for the accident, the Duke of York granted Foote a licence to erect and run a theatre in Westminster for the rest of his life. Foote bought the old Haymarket Theatre, demolished it and built a new one on the site. His profligate lifestyle continued however, losing the best part of £2,000 in a gambling swindle whilst on a visit to Bath. Foote died in 1777 at Dover whilst on a journey across the Channel. Even his funeral was somewhat bizarre, being buried by torchlight in Westminster Abbey. Perhaps his most famous contribution to the English language is the phrase 'The Grand Panjandrum', from a nonsense verse he wrote as part of another war of wit, this time with Charles Macklin.

Furniss, John Cooper

In 1875 master baker John Cooper Furniss opened a teashop in Truro. His specialities were gingerbread biscuits and fairings, which he baked in the early hours before the teashop opened. The name 'fairing' was originally applied to a

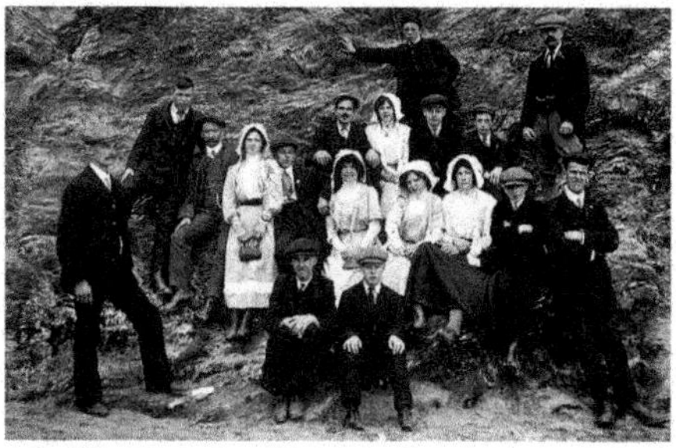

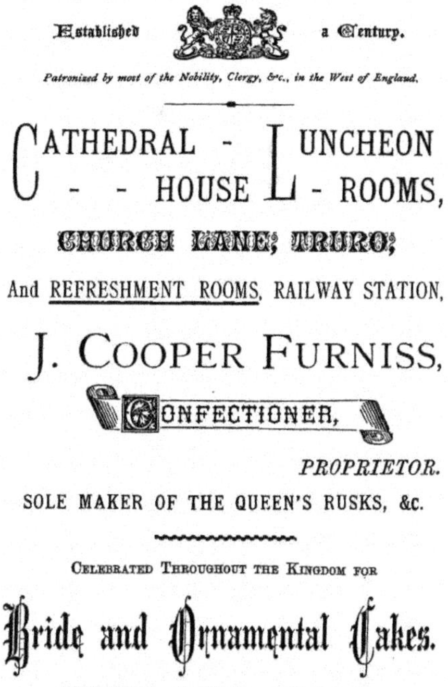

(*Left*) staff from Furniss factory celebrate the company's twenty-fifth anniversary in 1911 (picture courtesy of Furniss Ltd) and (*right*) an advertisement from 1883.

small gift of sweets bought at a fair, usually for a sweetheart. When the cathedral foundation stone was laid by the Prince of Wales on 20 May 1880, Furniss was chosen to provide lunch, and such was his enterprise that afterwards he even sold copyrighted photographs of the event at a shilling each. He also sold his refreshments at the newly opened railway station, and claimed royal patronage as sole maker of the Queen's rusks. It seems he enforced his own security, and when catering for a tennis club ball in September 1880 he was almost thrown down the stairs by a gentleman to whom he had refused entry. Both Furniss and his assailant brought charges of assault against each other, but those against Furniss were dismissed by the magistrates.

The son of a master baker, Furniss purchased land at Duchy Wharf and built a factory to produce his biscuits and sweets in larger quantities. He also expanded his range of products and started to sell by mail order. In 1886 he drew up an agreement to sell his business to the newly formed Furniss & Co. Ltd, retaining 800 shares in the new company. He also undertook not to carry on biscuit manufacturing in competition with the new company. The factory remained in Truro until 1988 when the business was relocated to Redruth. The iconic tins in which the biscuits are sold were supplied by the Barnsley Canister Company, and were decorated with a map of Cornwall. In keeping with the original definition, the fairings inside became a popular present to take home after a holiday in the county, as the family of the celebrity chef Rick Stein did when he was a child.

John Furniss died in 1888 at the age of fifty-five. He had been ill for some time, and died suddenly after experiencing difficulties swallowing an oyster. An inquest

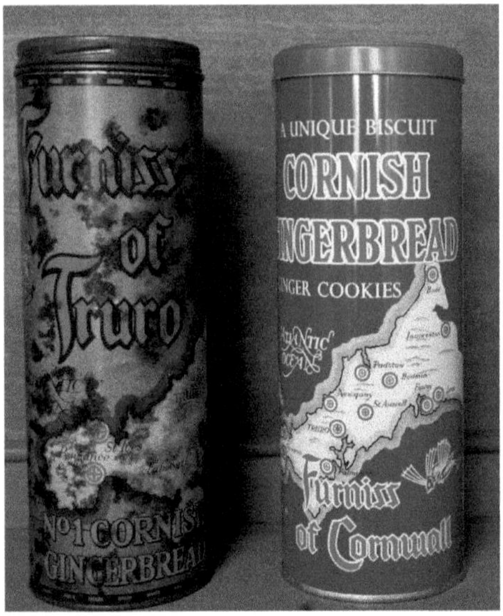

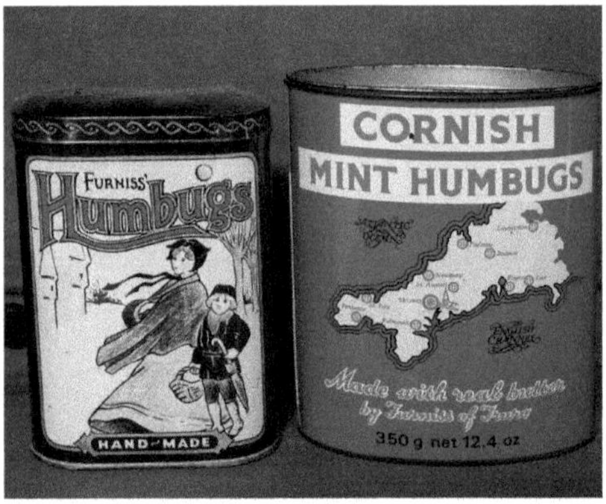

Some of the iconic tins of Furniss biscuits and sweets.

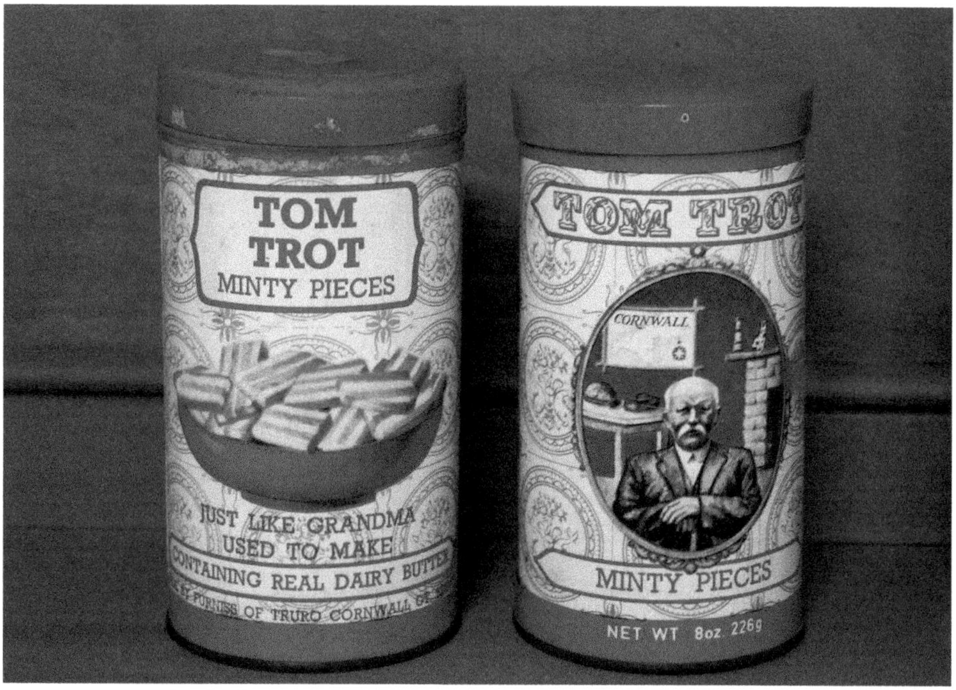

Furniss' Tom Trot tin has a picture of Richard Granville, who was injured during the construction of Truro Cathedral.

returned a verdict of accidental death. He was also a philanthropist, in his will leaving 100 shares in the factory to set up the Furniss Coal Fund, the income from which was to be used to buy coal for disadvantaged parishioners in the city. The scheme is administered today by Truro City Council who still distribute Furniss tickets in the early autumn which can be exchanged by deserving parishioners for bags of coal to use during the winter months.

When in 1908 Richard Granville lost both legs in an accident working on the new cathedral, the company supported his family through sales of Furniss's mint-flavoured Tom Trot sweets, paying a royalty from every tin sold, and even printing a portrait of Mr Granville on the tin. The name Tom Trot or Tam Trot for a type of butterscotch was commonly used in Victorian times and the recipe is likely to go back much further.

Furniss Island

Adjoining the site of the old factory, this small island between the banks of the River Allen has become a recreation area and has been laid out as a small park. It is looked after by a group calling themselves the Friends of Furniss Island with some financial help from the company whose name it bears.

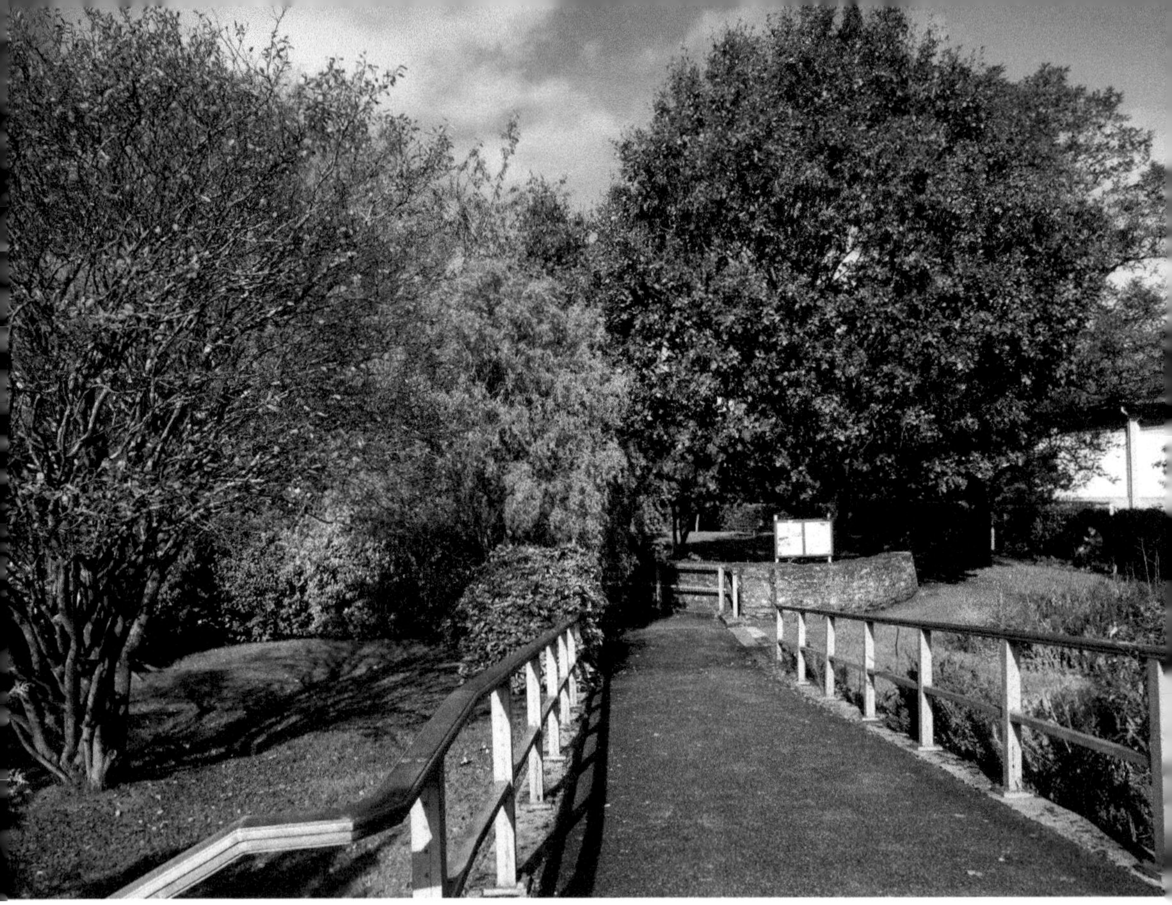

Above and below: Furniss Island.

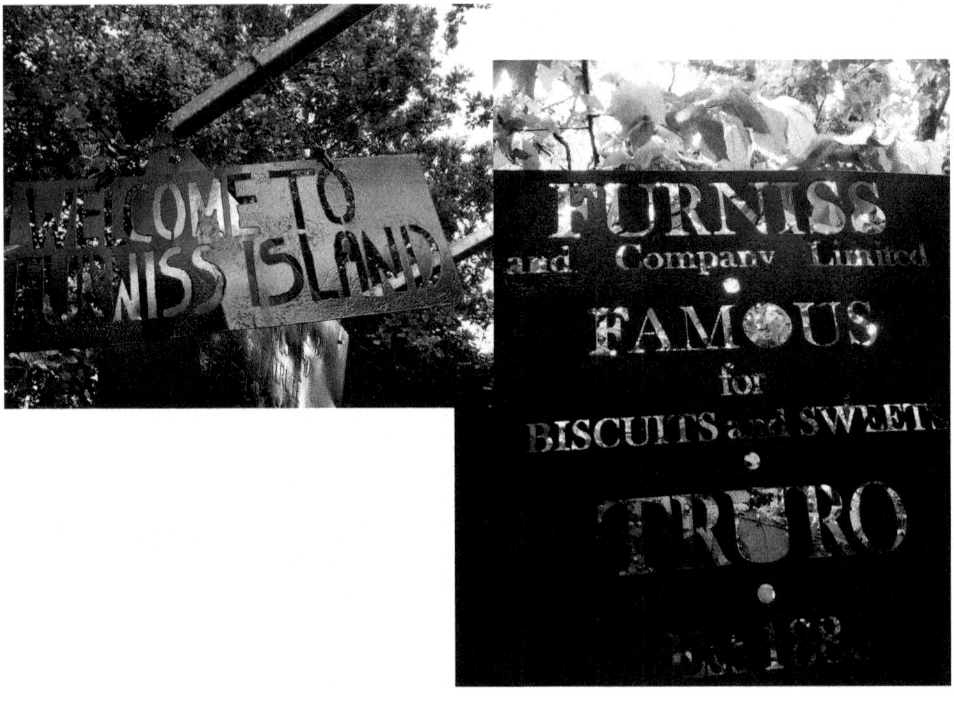

Furniss, Harriet Maud

The second daughter of John Cooper Furniss, Harriet (known as Maud) was born in Truro in 1866 and at the age of twenty became a scholar at Newnham College, Cambridge, a ladies' college founded in 1871. In 1889 she was awarded an *aegrotat* degree in mathematics. This meant that due to illness she was unable to take the exam, instead receiving a degree reflecting her expected level of attainment. In April 1890, she obtained a post as one of four lady computers employed by the Royal Observatory, Greenwich. The observatory had taken delivery of several new telescopes and needed extra computing staff to analyse the transits of stars which were recorded on photographic plates. As a result of her work she became one of the first female members of the British Astronomical Society. However, in January 1891 she resigned and returned to live with her widowed mother, also called Harriet, at Lemon House in Truro. The following year she took up a post as an assistant mistress at Orme Girl's School in Newcastle-under-Lyme. She remained in Staffordshire until 1907 when she returned to Plymouth to look after her older sister's family following her death, and remained there until her own death in 1949.

G

Gourzong, Claude

Friday 14 July 1967 was a fateful day for one of Truro's most historic buildings, but without the actions of a heroic lorry driver it could have been much worse. At around 11.15 a. m. a lorry laden with 8 tons of concrete blocks started its descent of the hill at the top of Lemon Street when its brakes failed. The driver, Claude Gourzong, a West Indian who had made his home in the county, used all his skill and courage to steer the runaway vehicle down the hill managing to avoid cars and pedestrians, sounding the horn and leaning out of the cab shouting 'my brakes have failed, keep clear!' At the junction with Boscawen Street, busy with shoppers, Mr Gourzong saw that the frontage of the historic Red Lion Hotel across the street was clear of pedestrians and steered his vehicle towards it. He demolished a set of traffic lights and sent a pillar box flying into the air before the vehicle hit the frontage of the hotel with such force that part of the building collapsed on top of his cab and trapped his left leg. By sheer good fortune, the front bar of the hotel was closed and the lounge above was empty, so there were no casualties inside the hotel. It took two hours for firemen to free Mr Gourzong's badly injured leg, as it turned out the only human casualty of the incident. Given that the traffic that morning was described as heavy, it was no surprise that his actions were hailed as most heroic by the police afterwards.

Apart from the street furniture, the only other casualty was the Red Lion itself: built in the late seventeenth century by a relative of Samuel Foote, it became an inn in 1769 and its half-timbered frontage was a much-loved feature of Boscawen Street. The damage it sustained that July morning proved to be terminal, however, and the following November it was demolished and replaced with a modern shopfront.

Green Fingers

These belong to the gardeners of the Parks and Gardens Department who look after the city's green spaces. Between 1974 and 2018 the City Council have won no fewer than thirty awards in the South West in Bloom Competition, including in 2018 being

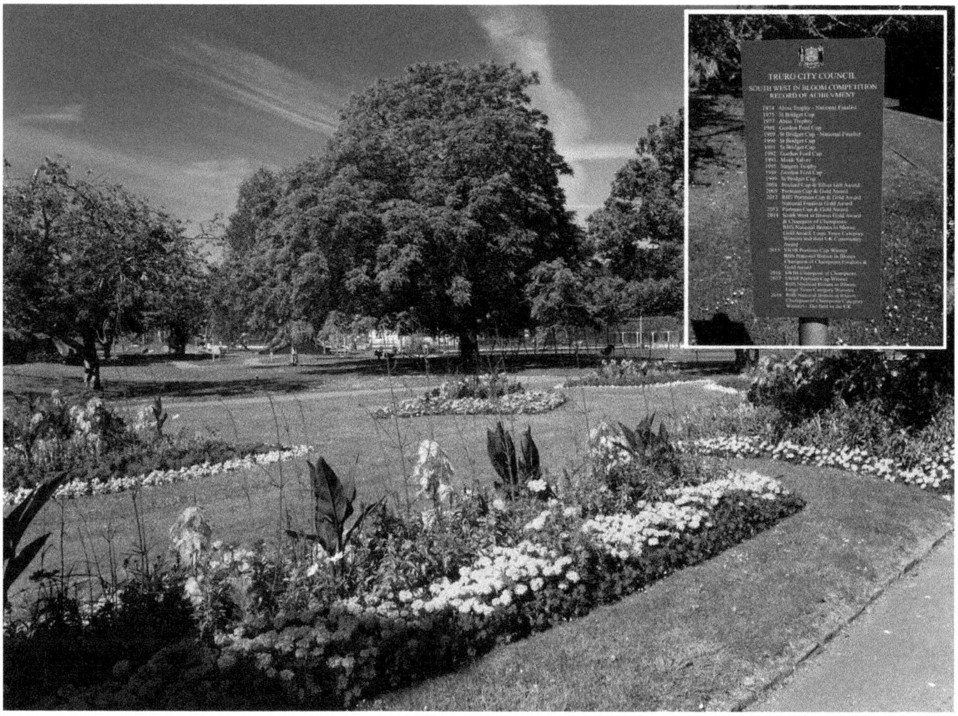

Boscawen Gardens and (*inset*) the list of horticultural awards won by the City Council gardeners.

crowned the RHS National Britain in Bloom Champion of Champions, the best in the UK. This magnificent record of achievement is displayed on a board in Boscawen Park, which lies beside the Truro River on the Malpas Road, on the opposite bank to Newham. There is an attractive gardens and recreation area, with an adjoining cricket ground.

'Guinea a Minute' Daniell

Born in 1715, Thomas Daniell went on to become one of the most successful mine owners in Cornwall. His copper mine at Porthtowan was so lucrative that it earned him his nickname. The eighteenth century was a boom time for copper mining in Cornwall, and Daniell started his career as a clerk to William Lemon. After Lemon's early death in 1760, Daniell purchased his mining interests. Thomas Daniell's son, Ralph Allen Daniell, continued the family fortunes after his father's death in 1793. He acquired the estate of Trelissick overlooking the River Fal (now in the care of the National Trust) after the previous owner had fallen into debt. Ralph's son, Thomas, eventually inherited Trelissick but the nineteenth-century downturn in mining (and perhaps his overspending on the estate) led to his bankruptcy in 1835. (See also Princes Street.)

H

High Cross

The area known as High Cross fronts the west door of the cathedral beside St Mary's Street. It is one of Truro's most attractive cityscapes. Particularly attractive is the Georgian former Assembly Rooms, built in the late 1780s and which boasted a theatre. The handsome pedimented front is still preserved adjacent to the west front of the cathedral. It is decorated with plaques containing cameos of Shakespeare and Garrick, although today these adorn the fronts of more mundane businesses. In the late nineteenth century, the fire station also fronted High Cross.

There is also an ancient Celtic cross, thought to be the borough cross of Truro, recorded as far back as 1290. It has a wheel-shaped head and part of its original shaft.

The Georgian Assembly Rooms façade, High Cross.

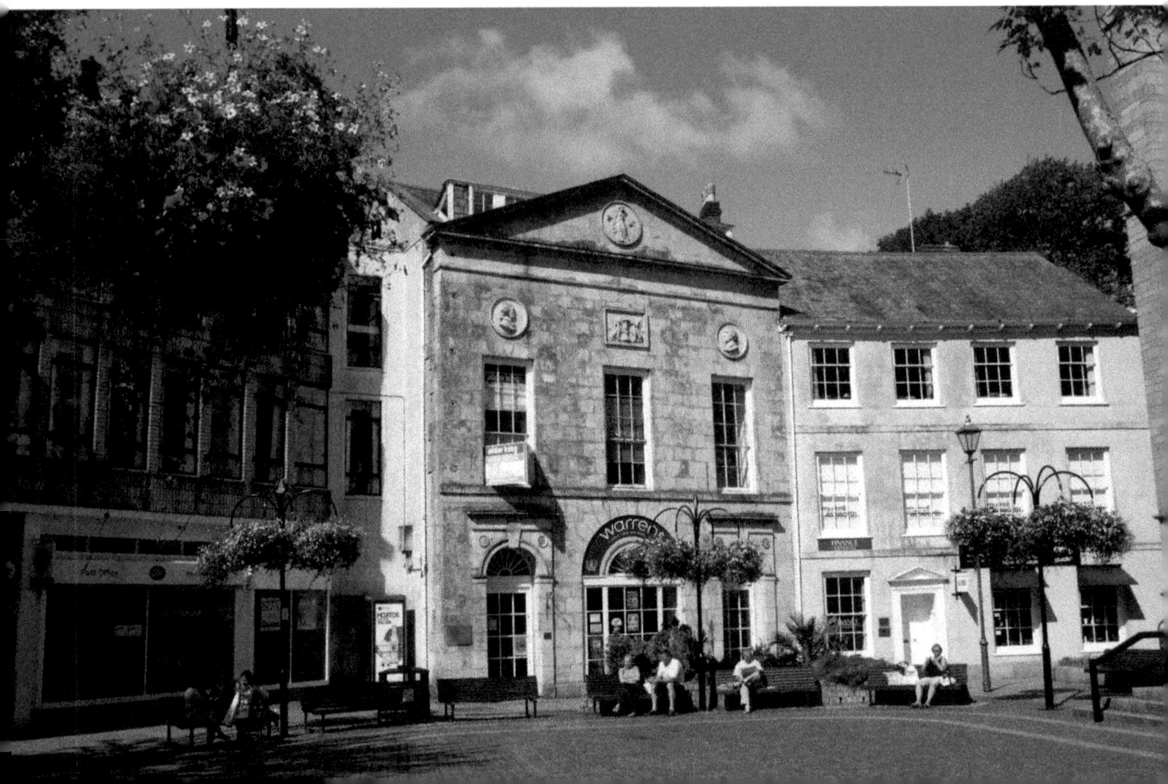

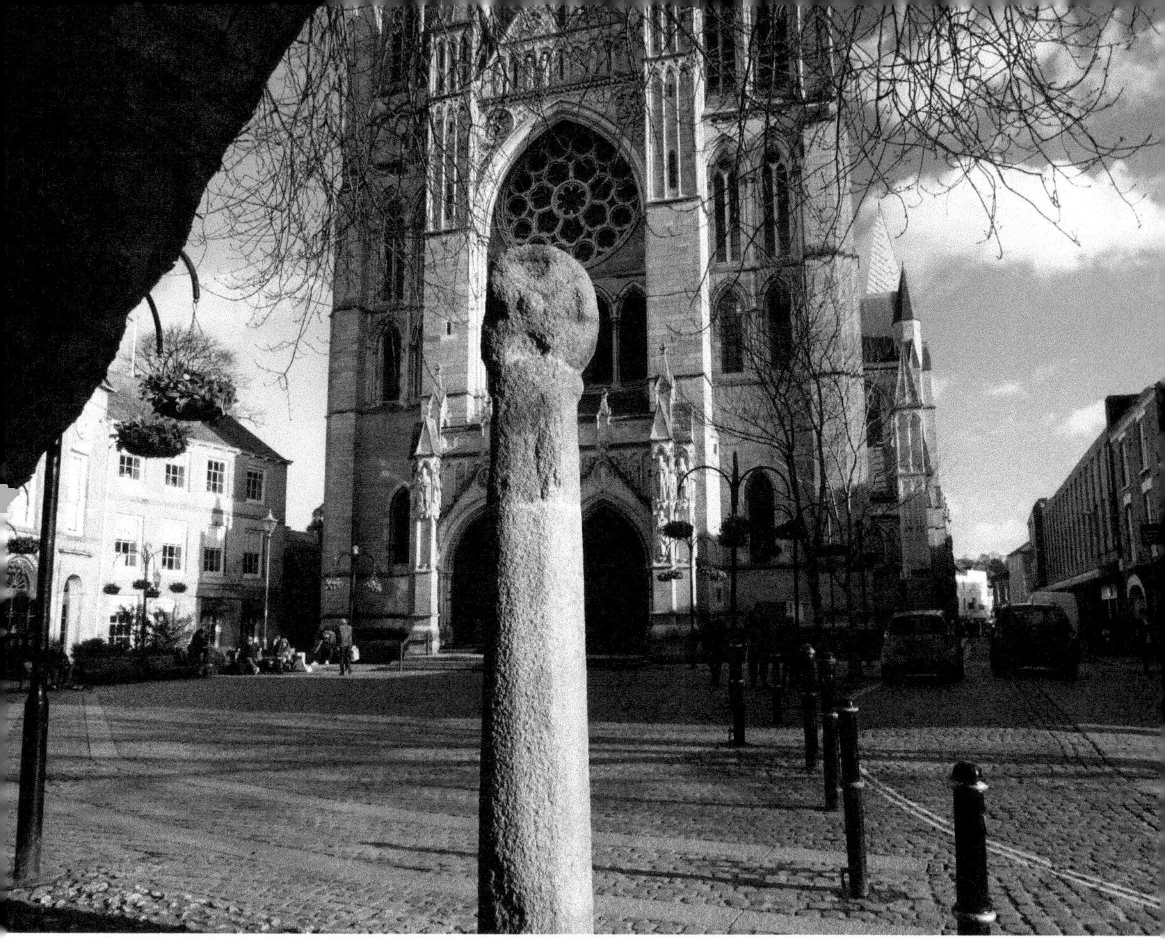

High Cross: the ancient cross dates from the thirteenth century.

The cross was found in the vicinity in 1958 by workmen digging a trench nearby, and was placed in its present position in 1988. A nineteenth-century record describes it having a base with a ring for bull-baiting, but this has been lost. In February 2019, the cross was removed for repair after it was damaged by a car, but stonemasons Ian and Alex Piper have repaired it and it is back in its rightful place.

H. T. P.

The letters H. T. P stand for Hosken, Trevithick & Polkinhorn. They are well known to Truronians of a certain age as they appear on a former riverside mill and once adorned a motor dealership on Lemon Quay. The Cornish conglomerate was created in 1890 by Sam Hosken and his nephew from W. Hosken & Son, two grandsons of the steam engine inventor Richard Trevithick of J. H. Trevithick & Sons, and Sam Polkinhorn, a businessman and wool merchant. He lived in Princes House, and was later to become mayor of Truro. They brought together Cornwall's finest flour mill, retailing and shipping at Hayle and numerous businesses, including Poltisco wharf, in Truro.

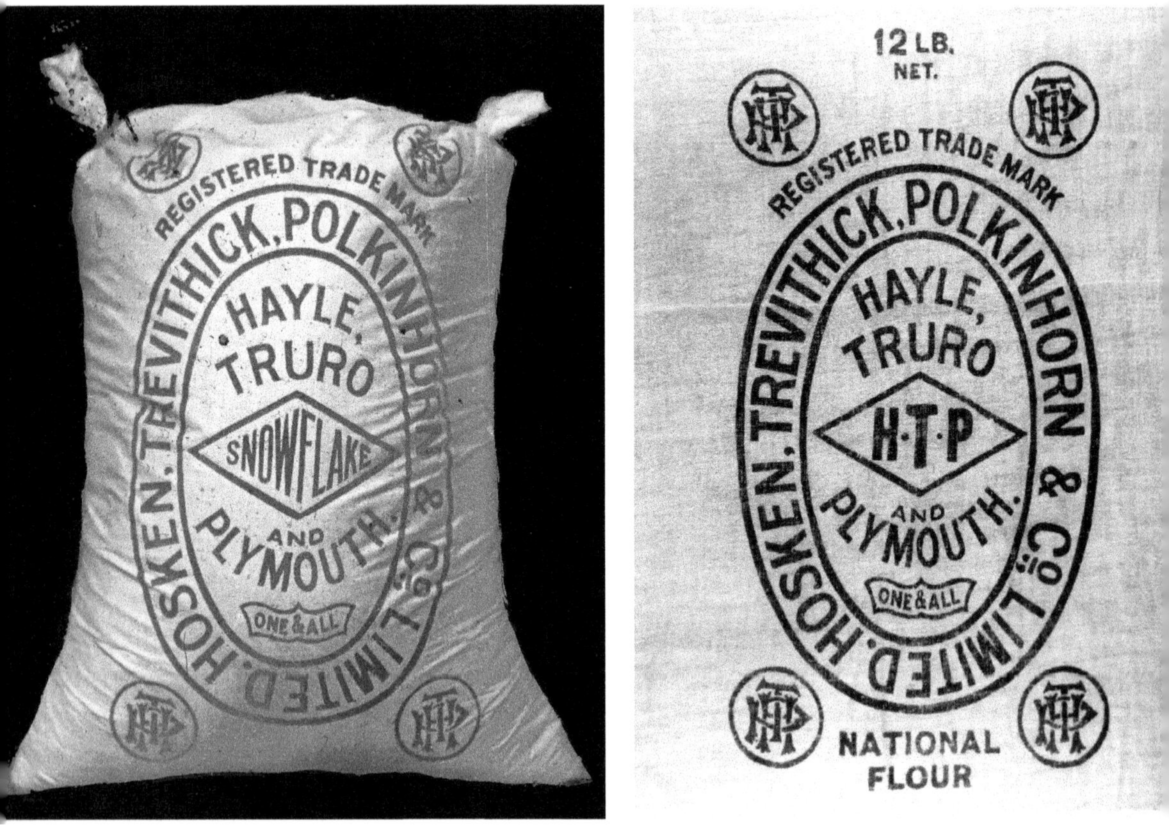

H. T. P. flour sacks. (Picture courtesy of Philip Hosken)

In 1911, the company completed building Poltisco Mill facing Truro River with the company's initials displayed in brick on the pediment. It also owned a large mill at Devonport, operated the Liverpool, Bristol and Hayle Steamship Company carrying passengers and freight on a weekly basis between these and other ports, and a large wool processing factory in Tavistock. Its main occupation was milling, which it continued until 1936 when Spillers Ltd purchased that side of the business with its H. T. P. name and goodwill. The remaining company carried on in agriculture as Farm Industries Ltd.

Its involvement in transport provided it with sufficient knowledge to create H. T. P. Motors, located in what is now the Wear House, Truro, in 1934. A fine garage, now the Pannier Market, was built on Lemon Quay in the gardens of Princes House in 1938. The building, business and its name were sold to Mumfords of Plymouth the following year. During the Second World War, they repaired Spitfires as well as maintaining vehicles. The Poltisco Mill was not sold to Spillers but occupied by Western Counties Agriculture until 1977. It then stood dormant, its reinforced concrete structure surviving as its neighbours crumbled, to be redeveloped in 1996 into the fine apartment block that stands today.

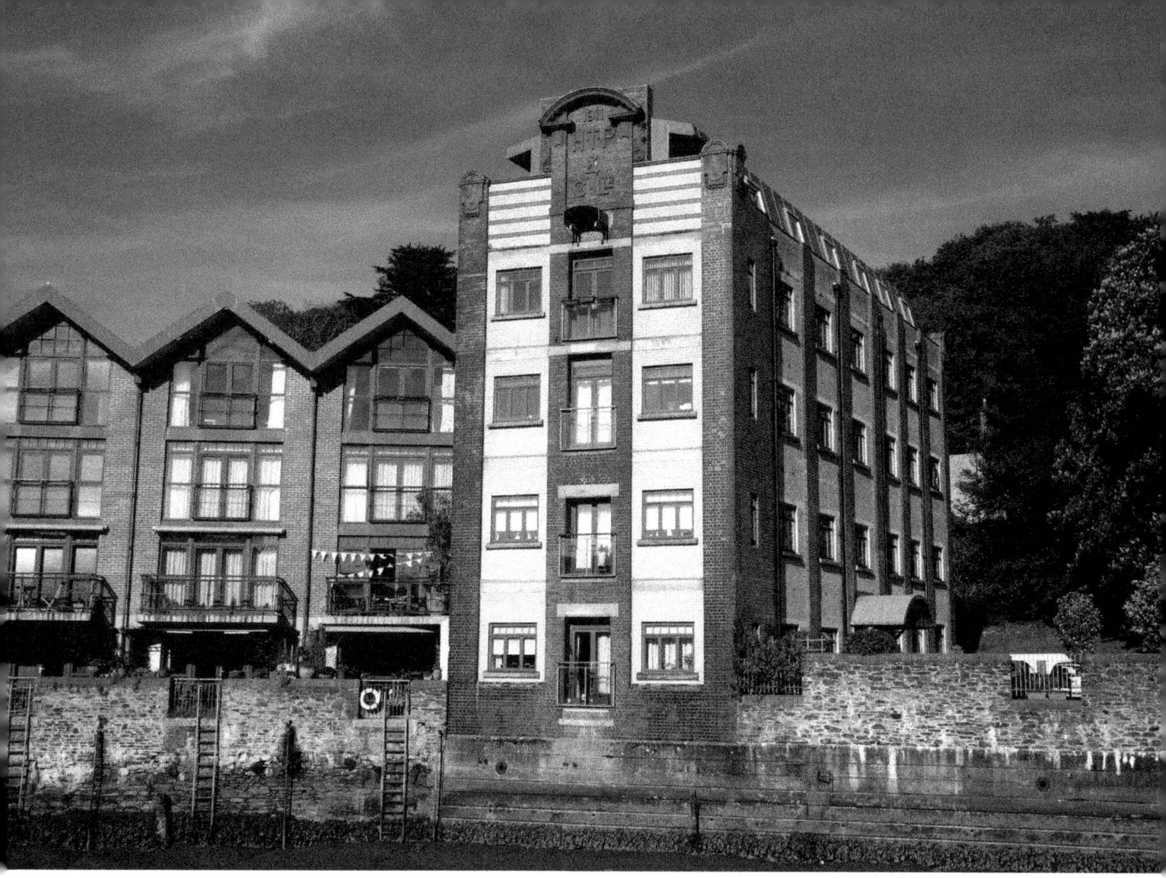

Above and below: The former H. T. P. mill building on Poltisco Wharf.

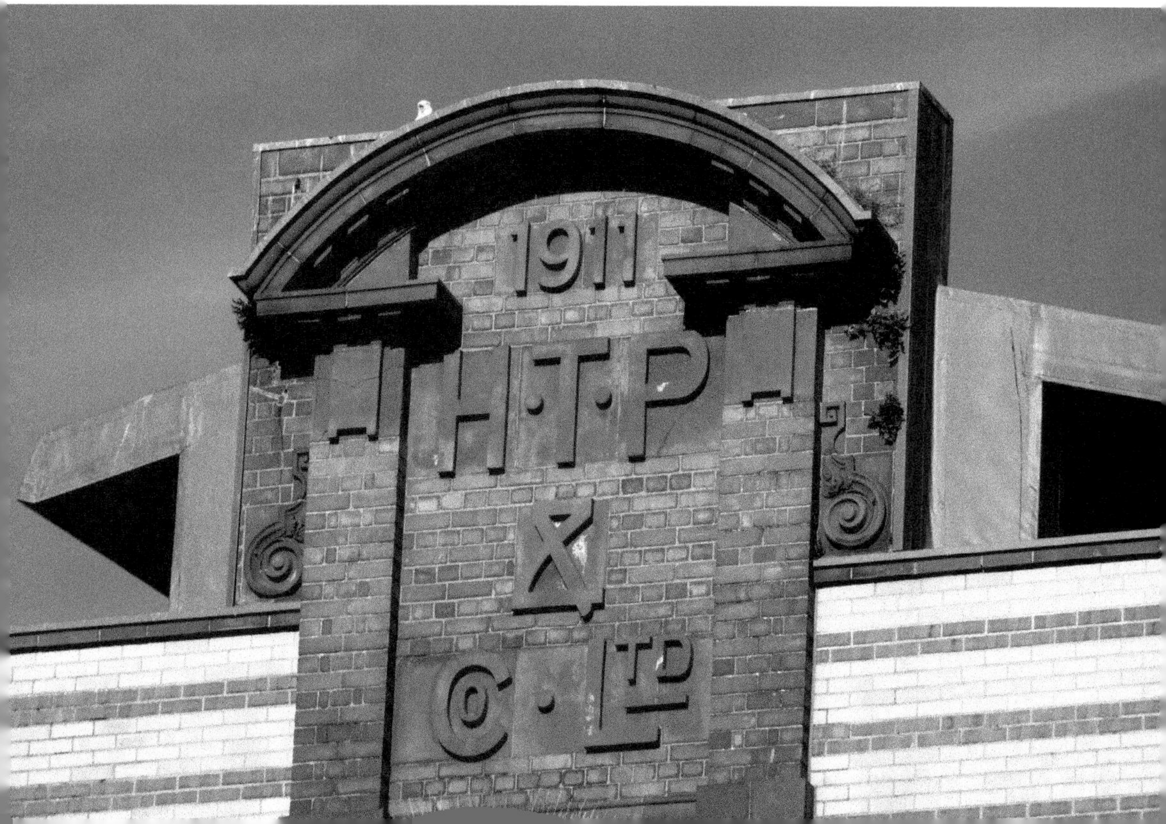

I

Idless

Just a mile to the north of Kenwyn along quiet lanes, the tiny hamlet of Idless borders the River Allen. Its name is nothing to do with laziness, deriving from Cornish *Edhelys*, meaning 'Place of Aspen Trees'. It consists of a manor house, a Gothic-style converted mission church, a row of cottages and some converted mill buildings. The manor was recorded in the Domesday Book when it was owned by Robert de Mortain. Scawswater Mill was built around 1850, on the site of an earlier fifteenth-century mill and has been used for grinding corn, fulling cloth and as a sawmill. There are also remains of a blowing house used to smelt tin.

In the late nineteenth century, the first Bishop of Truro, Edward White Benson, who lived at the nearby bishop's palace (now Epiphany House), was in the habit of taking his family out for 'a long vague walk' in the direction of Idless. Tagging along would be his daughter's goat, Tan. Also with them was Benson's son, Arthur Christopher, who would later write the words 'Land of Hope and Glory' to Elgar's famous tune, and his younger brother Edward Frederic, who went on to write the Mapp and Lucia novels as well as lots of ghost stories.

The mission church at Idless.

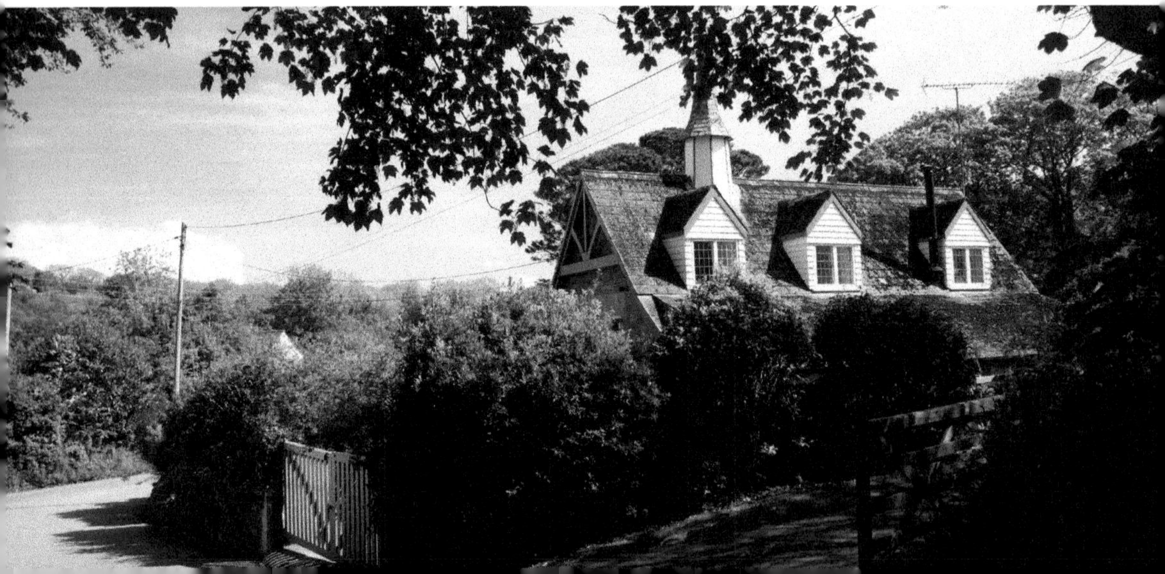

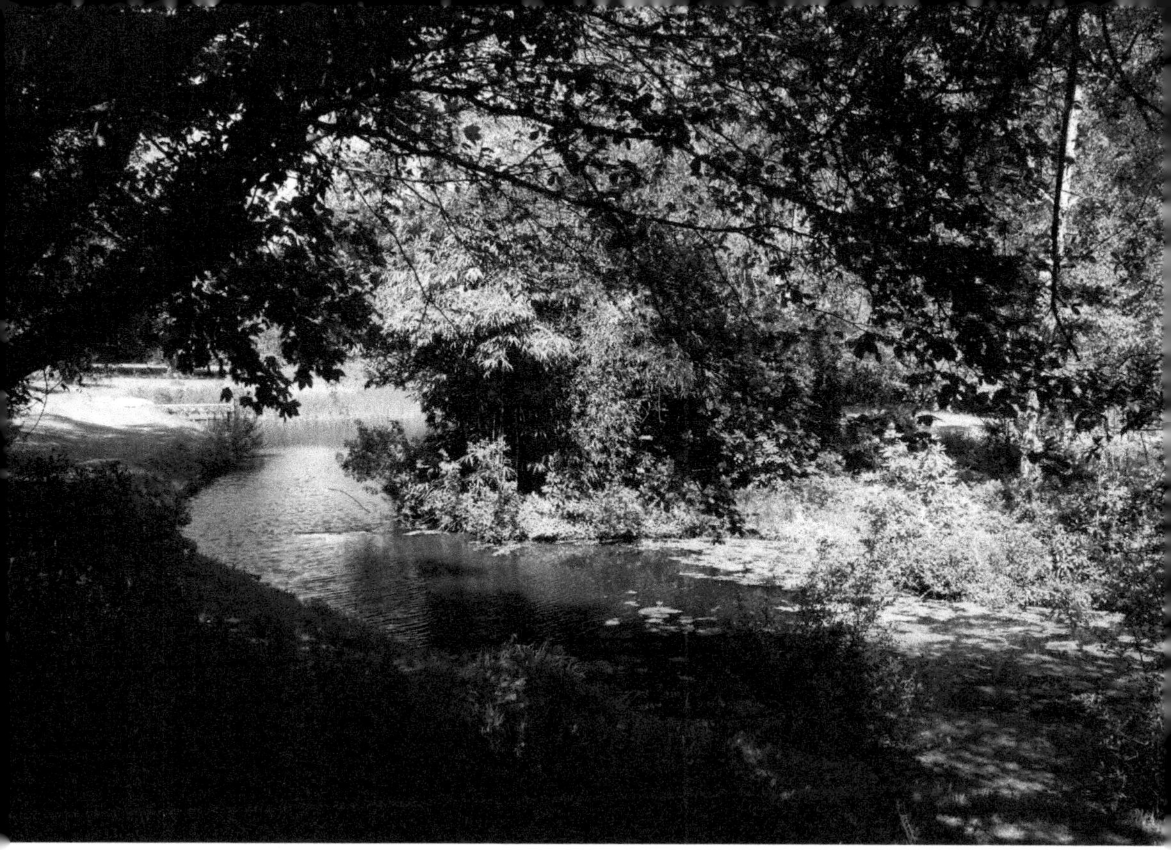

Above: The River Allen at Idless.

Below: Scawswater Mill, Idless.

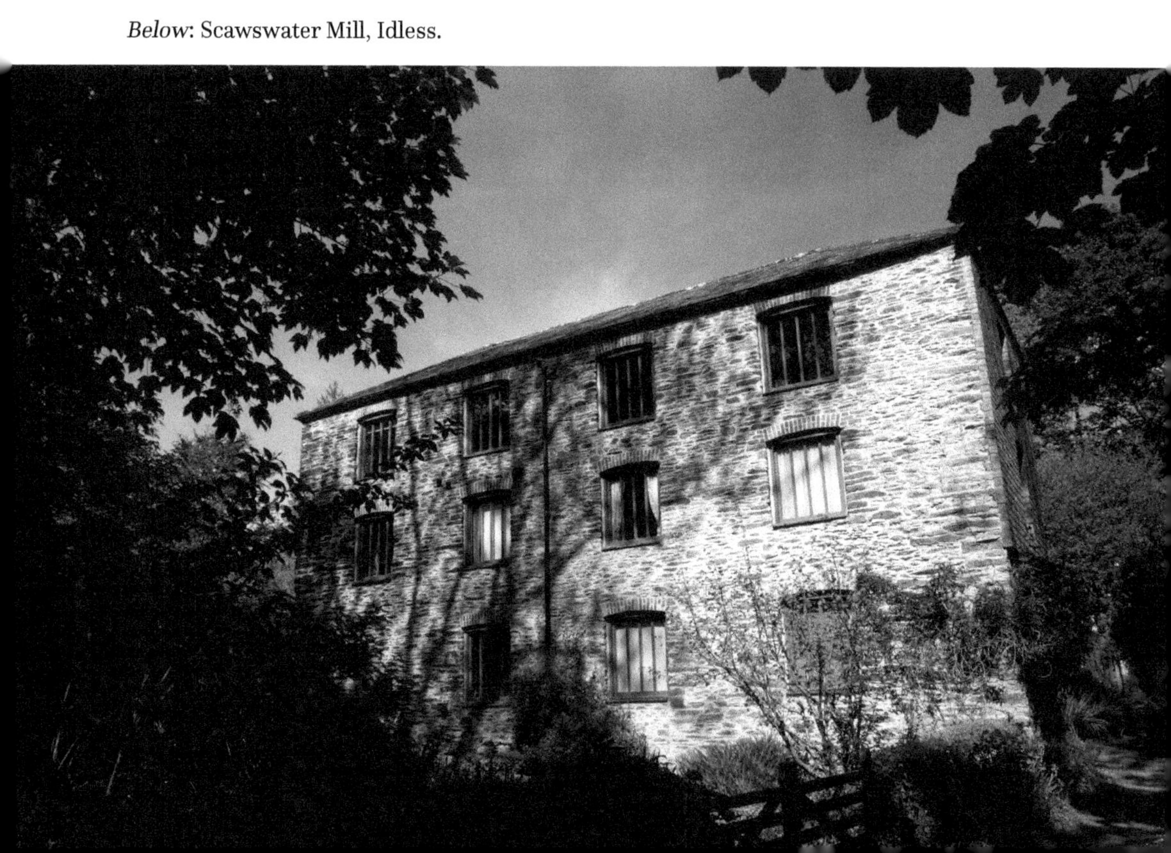

J

Jaws

Truro does have a connection with the film *Jaws*: the actor Robert Shaw, who played shark hunter Quint in the film, attended Truro School after the family moved to Cornwall from Lancashire following his father's death, when Shaw was twelve. In fact, his parents had met and married in Truro in 1926 when his father was working as a doctor and his mother training as a nurse. Robert started at the school in 1939 and proved to be good at sports, especially sprinting, winning the *Victor Ludorum* in 1945. He was made Head Boy and he also excelled at rugby, playing for Camborne Town in 1947. At Truro School his acting talent was quickly recognised and he took part in drama productions, playing roles as diverse as Mark Antony and Peter Pan. His acting was so gripping that he sometimes scared the boys in the audience. After he left, he won a place at RADA and went on to play small roles in many famous films, including *The Lavender Hill Mob* and *The Dambusters*. Casting *Jaws*, director Stephen Spielberg had to convince Shaw he was right for the part, as Shaw had read the book and hated it. As well as *Jaws*, he starred in many big-budget films, including *From Russia with Love*, *The Taking of Pelham 123*, *The Sting*, and *Force 10 from Navarone*. He revisited Truro School as an old boy in the 1960s.

K

Keam, Thomas Varker

By a happy coincidence whilst exploring the churchyard at Kenwyn, I came across a gravestone bearing the inscription 'In affectionate remembrance of Thomas Varker Keam, late lieutenant of the United States' Army and Keams Cañon, Arizona, died at Truro, 30th November 1904.' Why would a US soldier with a canyon named after him be buried in Truro? A quick Internet search revealed that Thomas Keam, who was born in Truro in 1842, emigrated to North America in 1862 and joined the Union army, later becoming an Indian trader among the Navajo and Hopi tribes.

The son of a ship's captain, Keam was born in Kenwyn parish and grew up in West Bridge Street, roughly where Victoria Square is today. He was the second of three children and attended school in Truro, leaving at fifteen to join the merchant navy. His voyages eventually took him via Australia to San Francisco. This was at the height of the American Civil War, and aged nineteen, Keam left his ship and joined the California Volunteers as a private of the Union army. Keam's unit's principal adversary was to be the Apache raiders they encountered on their desert marches east towards New Mexico and Texas. After the Civil War ended, Keam left the Californians and joined the New Mexico Volunteers as a Second Lieutenant, serving under the famous Colonel 'Kit' Carson, setting up reservations to help manage what the government called the 'Indian problem'.

After being discharged from the military in 1866, Keam, who was known as Keams in the US, spent the next decade working for the government's Indian Bureau among the native tribes of Arizona, learning the Navajo and Hopi languages and acting as an interpreter. He gained respect among the Navajo because he was trustworthy and fair. Around this time his younger brother William joined him in Arizona also as an interpreter. In 1869, working in the reservation at Fort Defiance, Arizona, Thomas married a Navajo woman named Asdzáán Libá, with whom he had two sons. His career stalled when the management of the reservations was transferred from the army to Presbyterian missionaries. Men married to native women were referred to as 'squaw men' and since his marriage was never Christianised, he was forced out amid accusations of immorality, which he fought against unsuccessfully for over a decade. To add to his worries, Keam received a letter telling him that his mother was ill and he was forced to return to Truro. After he had been away for over a year, Asdzáán, thinking that he was not coming back, moved away, obtained a divorce and remarried, taking their sons with her. When he eventually returned, Thomas began a career as an independent trader, having established two trading posts in Arizona, one of which became known as Keams Canyon. It was run by William Keam until his early death in 1880, after which Thomas set up home there. Trading was frequently a form of barter, Keam supplying food and materials in exchange for handicraft work.

Thomas Keam's contribution to our western understanding of native American culture cannot be overestimated. He was the first trader to realise the cultural value of Navajo and Hopi art and craft pieces, even making suggestions to enhance the saleability of their work. He used his marketing flair to develop contracts with curators and anthropologists and supplied large collections of ceramics, textiles and ceremonial art to the Smithsonian Institute and the Peabody Museum as well

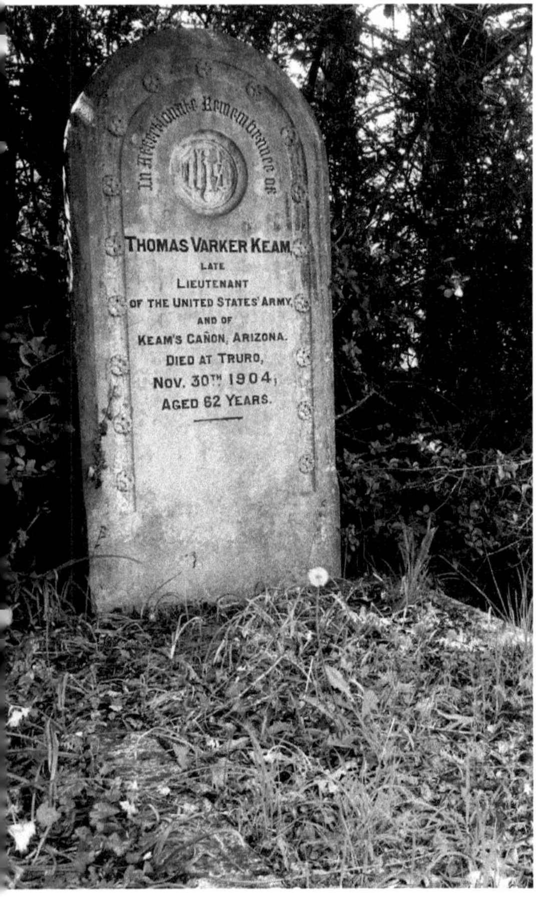

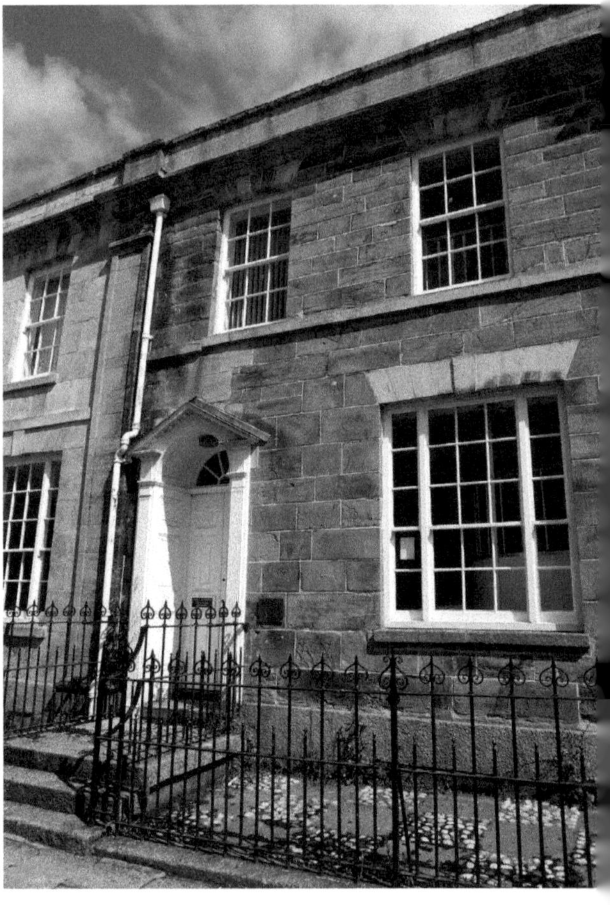

(*Left*) grave of Thomas Varker Keam, Kenwyn churchyard, and (*right*) No. 21 Lemon Street, where he died.

as further afield to the Berlin Museum of Ethnology. He did not forget his home city and donated a small collection of Navajo silver to the Royal Institution of Cornwall Museum. He also represented the Navajo and Hopi in negotiations with the government in Washington over what they termed 'civilising programmes', a role in which he either met or corresponded with every US president from the end of the Civil War to the end of the century. He kept an open house at Keams Canyon, offering hospitality to poor natives and distinguished academics alike. Among them was the Scottish anthropologist Alexander MacGregor Stephen, who lived at the canyon from 1882 until his death in 1894, and whose manuscripts and artefacts Keam took care to preserve after his death. It is gratifying to learn that Keam's two sons also visited him there.

In 1902 Thomas Keam, by now a sick man, sold his interests in the canyon and spent some time in Atlantic City for the good of his health, which improved enough for him to travel to Europe. Taking in France, Italy and Switzerland, he returned to Truro for Christmas and advised on the display of the Rashleigh mineral collection at the museum. After a further trip back to the US to manage his mining interests, in 1904 he returned for the last time to what he referred to as the old-fashioned but picturesque little city of his birth, living at No. 21, Lemon Street, where he died from angina. The trading post at Keams Canyon has now become McGees Indian Art Gallery and is still very much in the business that Thomas Keam began. Keam's obituary described him as 'a man of the highest integrity, widely read, cultivated and accomplished'. All the more surprising then that save for a few pieces of Navajo silver, he is almost unknown in his home city.

St Keyne Church, Kenwyn

The church at Kenwyn is thought to be the original mother church of Truro. In the twelfth century it was part of the manor held by Richard de Lucy, who built the castle. The present church dates from the fourteenth century, with the tower built a century later. In the early ninteenth century the church was in poor condition and was restored by Richard Polwhele. The tower was struck by lightning in 1860, leading to further restoration work. The lychgate with its attractive slate-hung schoolroom dates from the thirteenth century when it may have been used as a priest's lodging. It was used as a schoolroom until the 1920s, when it was restored. Today it is used as a meeting room.

Outside the porch we find a holy well dating from the fourth century, with nineteenth-century granite steps and posts and a vault. Inside the church there is Victorian stained-glass in memory of the Carlyon and Vivian families. The large churchyard is maintained as a wildlife haven (designated a living churchyard) and contains the graves of Joseph Emidy and Thomas Keam (see separate entries). The church's importance can be judged from the former vicarage, which dates from 1780

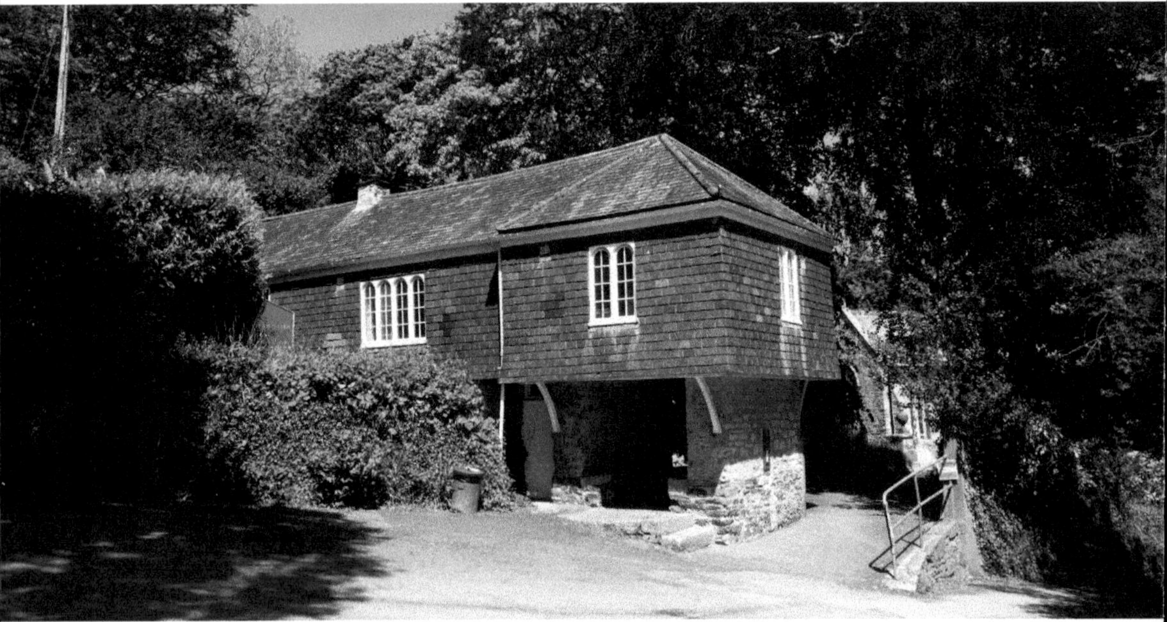

Above: The thirteenth-century lychgate at Kenwyn.

Below: The fifteenth-century tower of Kenwyn church and (*inset*) St Keyne's Well.

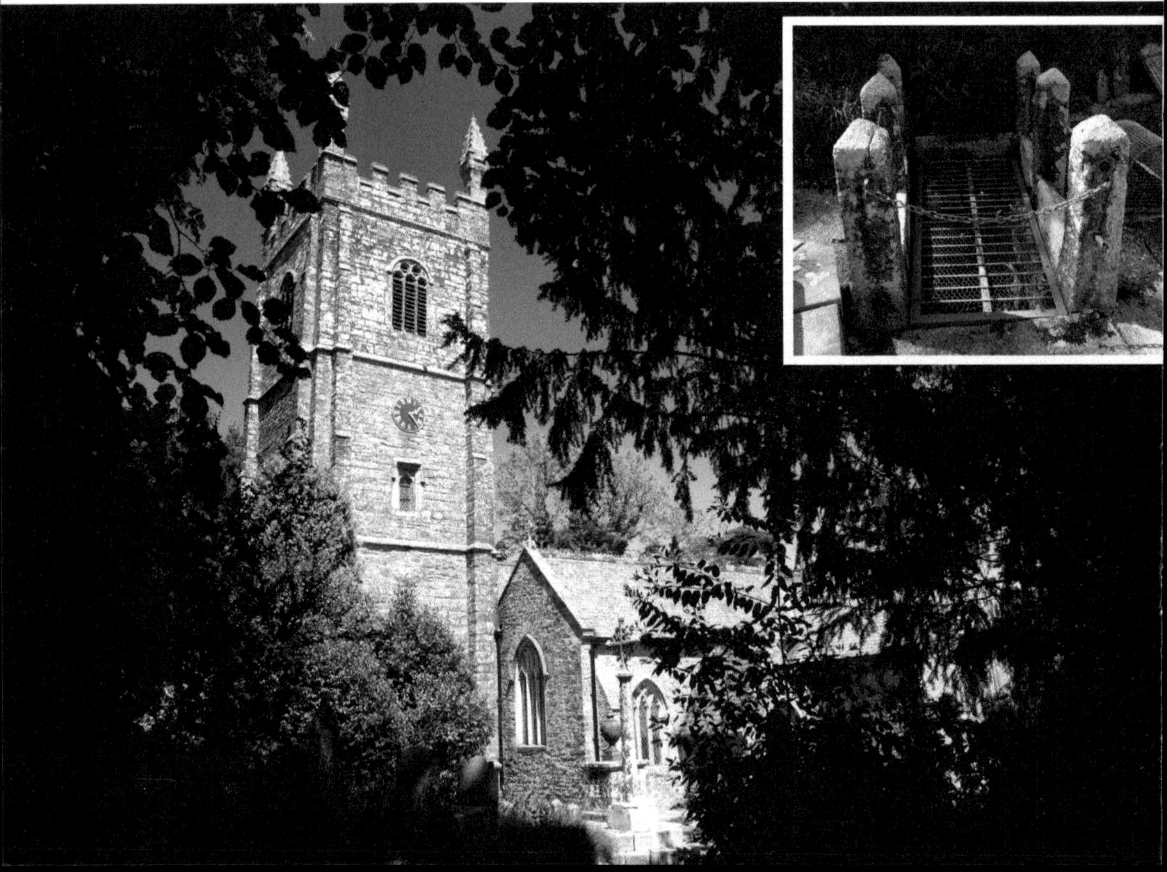

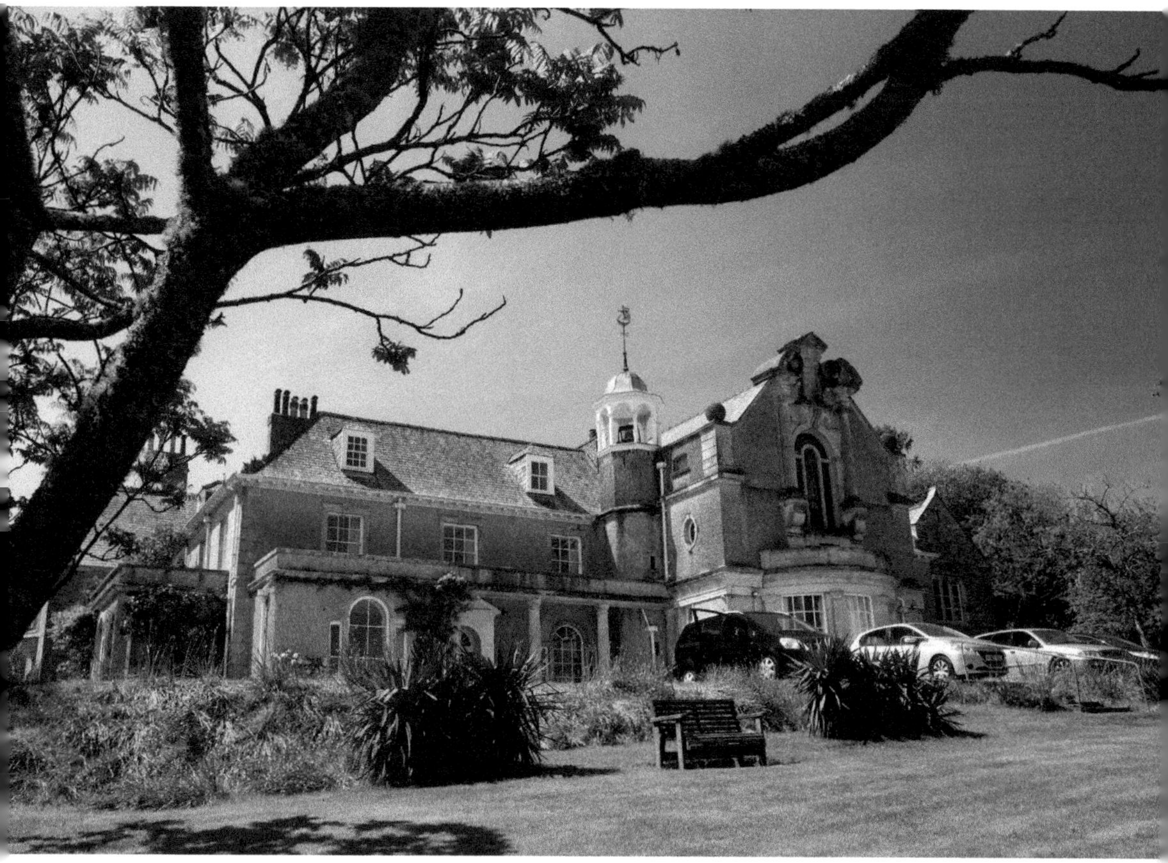

Epiphany House, once a vicarage and Truro's first bishop's palace.

and is now named Epiphany House. It became the first bishop's palace (*Lis Escop* in Cornish) in 1877. In the 1920s the house became home to a branch of the Community of the Resurrection, to which the bishop, Walter Frere, belonged. His was a somewhat controversial appointment as he was perceived as having strong left-wing sympathies and was well-known as a leading Anglo-Catholic. In the late 1920s, Frere became a focus for the controversy around a revised prayer book which had been approved by the House of Lords but rejected by the Commons. Some protestant Cornish clergy were suspicious of Frere's plans to introduce the controversial book into his diocese and in November 1929 a group of some 200 people marched through the city to Lis Escop singing hymns and carrying banners calling for Frere to resign. He stayed on until his health deteriorated in 1934.

In 1953, a smaller palace was built near Feock and Lis Escop was renamed Copeland Court, becoming home to Truro Cathedral School. In 1984 it became the new residence of the sisters of the Community of the Epiphany (see separate entry) when they moved from Alverton Manor. When the last two sisters moved away in 2001, it was renamed Epiphany House and became a Christian retreat and conference centre.

River Kenwyn

The Kenwyn could be called the secret river, as for most of its journey through the city it flows underground. In the early nineteenth century River Street was created by funnelling the river below ground as far as Lemon Quay, which was then a thriving port. Later in the twentieth century this too was covered over to form what is now a piazza. The river flows beneath the museum building, but can be followed upstream from the Leats towards Victoria Gardens and out of the city towards its source near Roseworthy. At Coosbean was a paper mill, described as moderately successful, which closed in 1839.

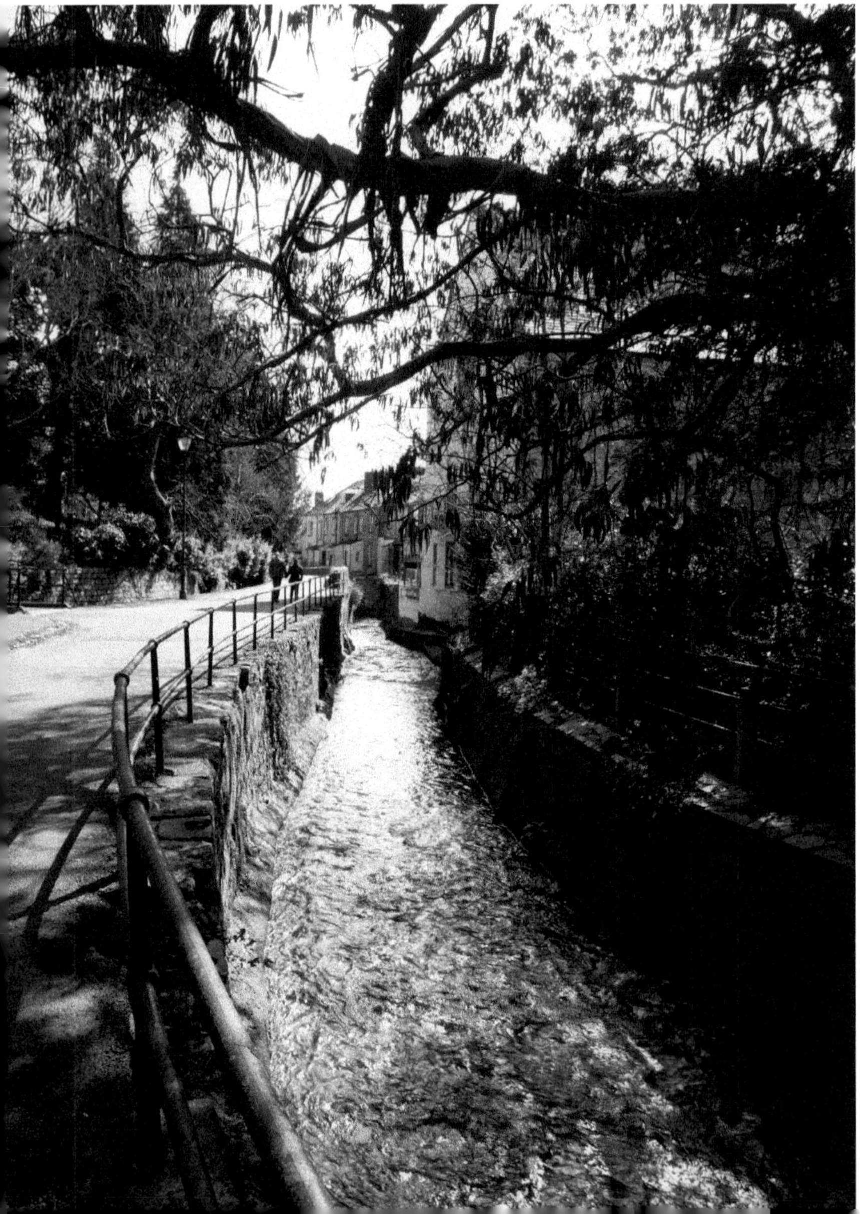

The River Kenwyn near Victoria Gardens.

L

Lander, Richard and John

Truro was the birthplace of one of England's most influential explorers whose low-born status meant that he is not much remembered outside of his home town and west Africa. Richard Lemon Lander was born in 1804 and his brother John in 1807. Their father was the landlord of the Fighting Cocks Inn, which was near Lemon Quay. The building, later renamed the Dolphin Inn, has since been demolished and all that remains is a plaque on the side wall of the Bishops Library in Green Street. He must have grown up hearing tales from the seafarers who came to drink in his father's hostelry, so that the urge to travel took hold at an early age. When he was only nine, he walked the 250 miles to London hoping to find an explorer who needed an assistant! When he was aged only thirteen, he joined the crew of a merchant ship and sailed to the West Indies. He contracted malaria in San Domingo, but this cloud had a silver lining because it gave him immunity from the disease, which was a distinct advantage in his later explorations of west Africa. Returning home, he worked in London as a servant to rich families, time which included some travelling in Europe. He then became a servant to the explorer Hugh Clapperton, travelling to South Africa in 1823 and west Africa in 1825. He was with Clapperton in Nigeria when his employer died, and returned to England the next year to break the news. Using Clapperton's journals, and his own diaries, he published two detailed accounts of the expedition. He returned to Truro, married and found a job at the Customs House, but the urge to travel was too strong and he volunteered to lead another expedition to explore the River Niger in 1830. He took with him his younger brother, exploring the length of the river on foot and by canoe, naming an island after his home town. When they reached the delta, the brothers were taken prisoner and a ransom had to be paid for their release. They travelled back via the island of Fernando Po and Rio de Janeiro in 1831. The brothers were invited to an audience with King William IV, and the Royal Geographical Society was so impressed by the results of the trip that in 1832 they awarded Richard their first ever Gold Medal. The citation was 'for important services in determining the course and termination of the Niger'. Richard Lander returned to Nigeria in 1833, without his brother, this time funded by a group of Liverpool shipping merchants who were hoping to establish trading posts on the river. This expedition was not a success, several of the party dying from fever early on. Eventually only nine members of the forty-seven-strong expedition returned to Britain. Lander was killed in 1834 whilst paddling upriver in his canoe, struck in his thigh by a musket ball. The ball went deep and although it was removed, he died of gangrene. He is buried on the island of Fernando Po (Bioko), and the musket ball is held in the Rotunda museum of artillery at Woolwich. His medicine chest is in the Royal Cornwall Museum in Truro. He left a widow and young daughter.

John Lander married a Truro girl and held various posts in Liverpool and London. He died in 1839 from a lung disease which it is speculated was a result of his travels in Africa. It is surprising that Richard Lander's story is so little known in Britain, yet in Nigeria it is part of the school curriculum. His expeditions opened up trade links between west Africa and the rest of the world, in particular the export of palm oil for which there was a growing demand for making soap.

More recently, the Richard Lander Society has been set up to foster British-Nigerian relations and in 2004, the 200th anniversary of his birth, an expedition was organised to explore the Niger following Lander's original route.

Lander Monument

Within a year of Richard Lander's death enough money had been raised by public subscription in Truro to erect a statue as a memorial. The statue was commissioned from Cornwall's greatest sculptor, Neville Northey Burnard, who grew up in Altarnun.

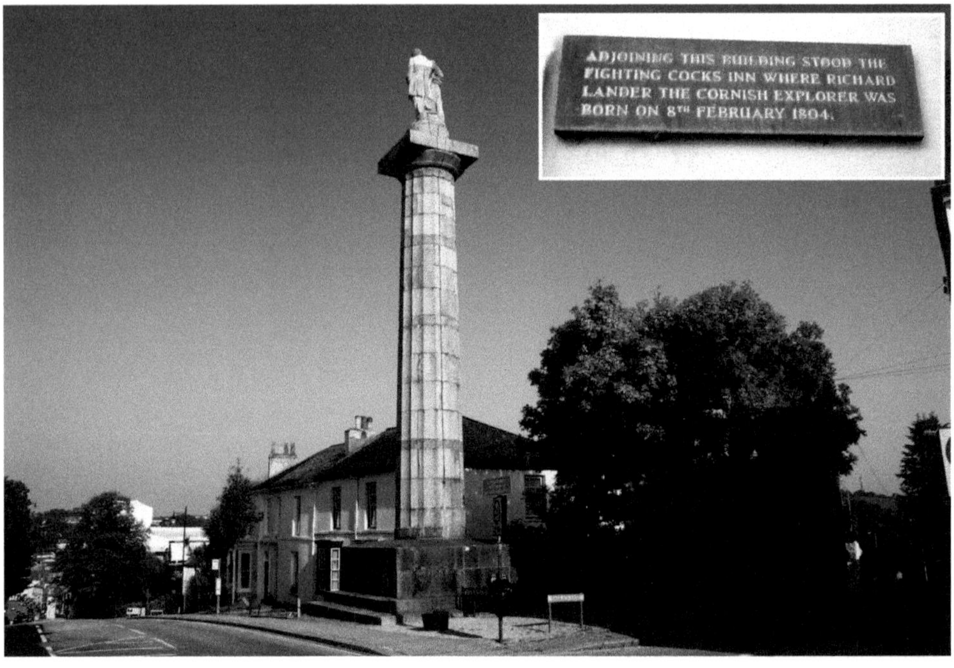

The Lander Monument in Lemon Street and (*inset*) plaque commemorating Lander's birthplace.

With the help of Sir Charles Lemon, his career took him away from this moorland village to London where his sitters included Edward VII, Gladstone and Thackeray, but his life ended in poverty in a Redruth workhouse after the death of his daughter led him to drink. He modelled the face of Lander on that of his young daughter who, it appears, inherited his features. The figure is holding a palm branch, said to be a symbol of peace and, maybe, the trade in palm oil. The statue was to be placed on top of a 60-foot-high Doric column designed by the prolific Truro architect Philip Sambell (see separate entry) who also designed St John's Church at its foot. The site, at the top of Lemon Street, was donated by Sir Charles Lemon. Construction began in 1835 but did not go entirely to plan when the column collapsed the following year, the result of poor workmanship and a lack of supervision. It was eventually completed in 1852. In 1934, an event to commemorate the centenary of his death was held around the monument, which was decorated with garlands for the occasion. 1,400 schoolchildren took part, a commemorative mug was issued, and Mrs Lander Johnston, Lander's granddaughter, was the special guest.

The city's most visible landmark after the cathedral adds a sense of scale to Lemon Street, and it is difficult today to imagine the view down the hill without it.

Leats

Truro's system of artificial water channels, known as leats, are the watery equivalent of its system of opes. In the twelfth century leats were cut to supply water to the timber castle (on the site of the County Court) recently built by Richard de Lucy. They also

Below and overleaf: The Leats near Victoria Gardens.

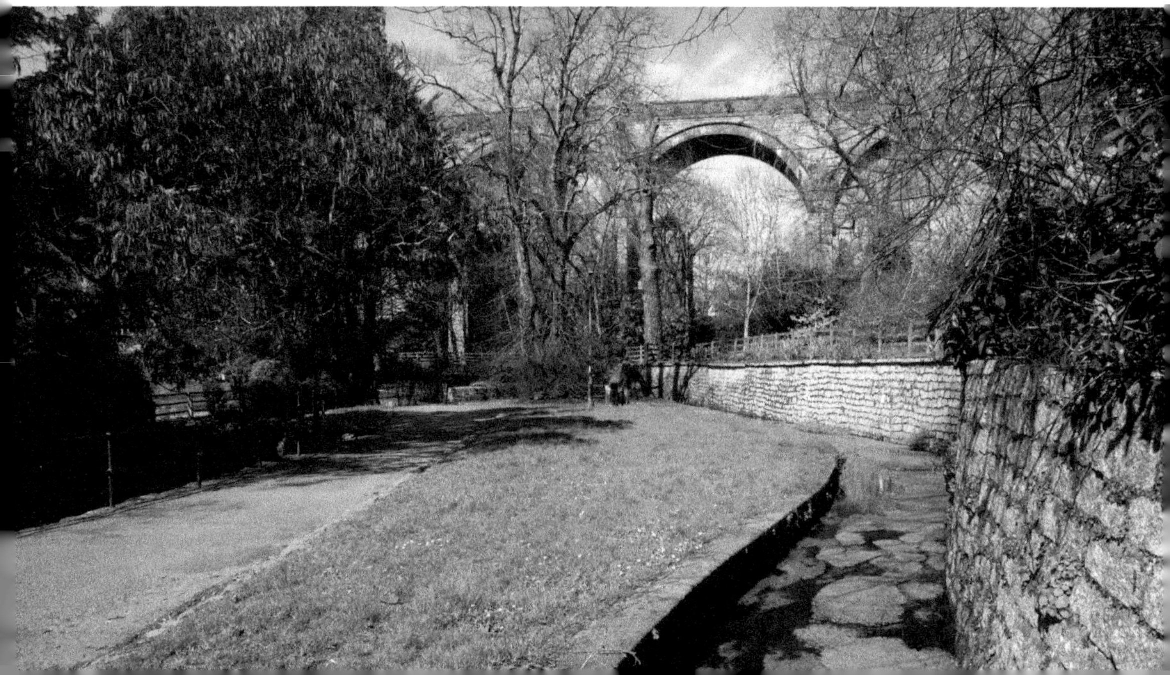

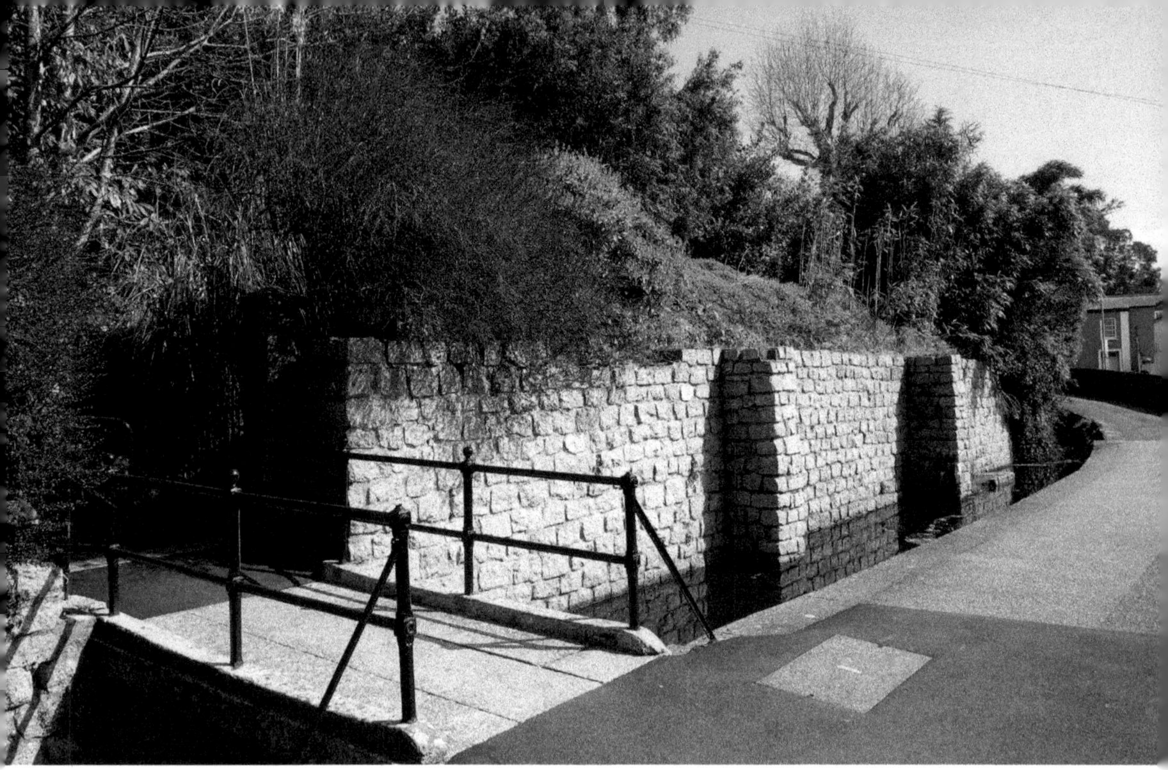

provided a water supply to power watermills, one of which was located in the area now occupied by Victoria Square. They were lined with granite and the best examples can be seen beside the path to Victoria Gardens leading off Castle Street beside the River Kenwyn, where there is still a sluice to control the flow of water through the system. In 1771, business owners who wished to be connected to the leat system were charged five shillings for the privilege, with the hatches through which their supply was channelled controlled by the grandly named Sergeant of Truro, Edward Bartlett. They also formed a key part of the city's drainage system, connected to narrower drainage gutters known as kennels which line the city streets to remove surface water. Most of the leat system today flows beneath the city and shoppers are blissfully unaware of its existence.

Lemon Family

This famous Cornish dynasty was founded by William Lemon, known as the Great Mr Lemon, who was born in West Cornwall in 1696. Sir Francis Basset said of him that 'he was a miner without a shilling, but by industry and good luck acquired £200,000'. From a relatively humble background, as a boy he took part in a human chain to rescue victims of a shipwreck. As a young man he became manager of a tin smelting works and in 1724 he married Isabella Vibert, who had inherited a substantial sum of money from her godmother. William used her dowry to finance his mining interests, initially at Wheal Fortune and then at Gwennap, near Redruth. Adopting the use of steam power invented by George Newcomen, he was the first mine owner to operate his mines on a large scale. He also owned the tin smelting works at Calenick. He was twice mayor of Truro and became County Sheriff. Lemon had Princes House built in 1739 and ten years later bought a country estate at Carclew, on the Falmouth road near Penryn, from the Bonython family for £3,300. He brought in the architect Thomas Edwards, who had designed Princes House, to oversee the completion of the estate. In later life he regretted his lack of a literary education and began studying under the tutelage of George Conon, headmaster of Truro Grammar School. Sir William owned a tame Cornish chough, which often accompanied him on his walks through Truro, and which would answer to his call. Unfortunately, one of the Grammar School boys, John Thomas, accidentally shot and killed the bird with his gun, and, much afraid duly confessed his crime to Mr Lemon. He was generously forgiven, and his misdeed never came to the attention of the headmaster. William Lemon's son predeceased him and after his death in 1760, the estate passed to his grandson, also called William. He became MP for Penryn in 1770 and in 1774, the year he was knighted, went on to represent the county until his death in 1824. He was responsible for the planning and building of Lemon Street. His eldest son William, an army major, shot himself in Hanover Square, London, at the age of twenty-five, in 1799.

Charles Lemon (1784–1868) inherited his father's titles after his death. Like his father he became MP for Penryn and later a Liberal member for West Cornwall. He was a strong supporter of science and technology who was elected a Fellow of the Royal Society in 1822, and was also a president of the Royal Statistical Society. In his home county he was president of the Geological Society of Cornwall, and was the first president of the Royal Polytechnic Society of Cornwall. As a memorial his name is carved on the wall of the Central Technical School, built in 1899 in Union Place, and his crest incorporated in stained glass inside. His life was beset by tragedy, losing his first-born son in childhood, and later his daughter at the age of only nine and his only other son at thirteen. Their deaths badly affected his wife and she died shortly afterwards. This left Sir Charles with no direct heirs, and on his death the estate at Carclew passed to his nephew. The house was destroyed by a fire in 1934.

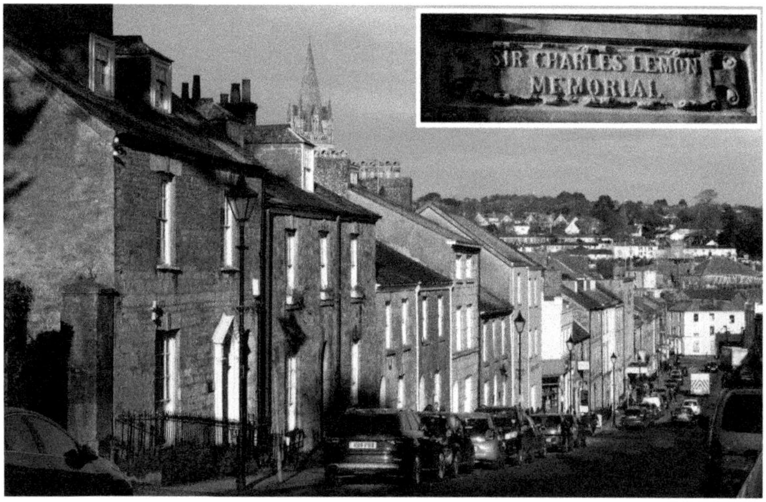

Lemon Street and (*inset*) memorial to Sir Charles Lemon in Union Place.

M

Mallets

This well-known hardware and homeware store in Victoria Square is one of the oldest retail businesses in Truro. In 1883 William Mallet began trading in the town of Fowey, selling hardware and ships chandlery. In 1897 he moved the business to Truro, acquiring premises in Victoria Square in 1911. William obtained one of his first buildings in an unusual way: he won it in a game of poker with the owner, Revd Enys! Sited in Walsingham Place, just behind his Victoria Square premises, it was used by Mr Mallet to store coffins, and the story goes that the men who made the coffins would sometimes sleep in them after a night on the town. When the shop girls came in to open up in the morning, they got quite a fright!

William's son Denzil joined the business in 1935 and, thirty years later, was succeeded by his son Robert. The last member of the family to run the firm, he sold the business in 2004. It is now owned by a national hardware chain, but still known to all its customers as Mallets.

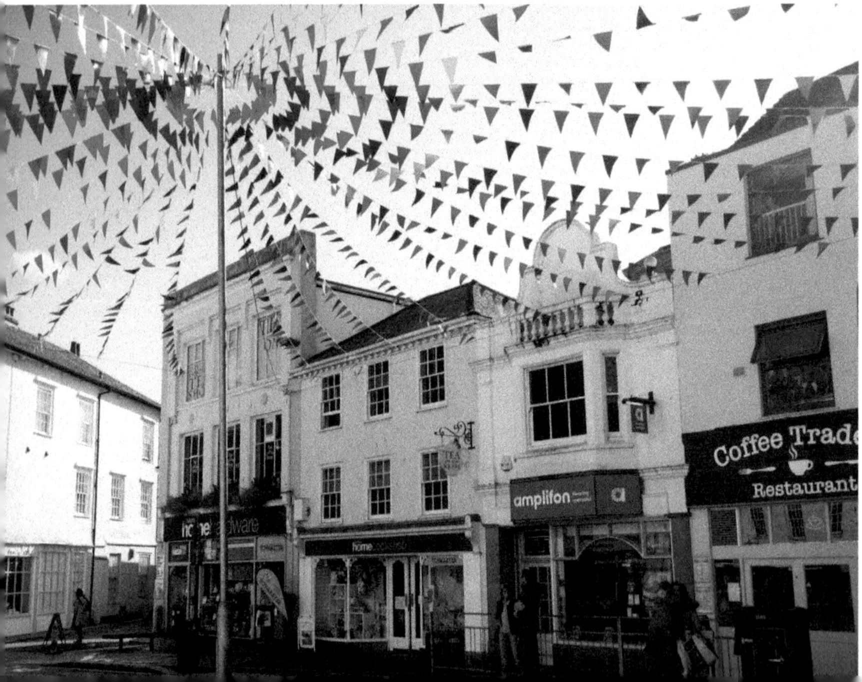

Mallets hardware store in Victoria Square.

Malpas

Situated at the confluence of the Truro and Tresilian rivers around a mile south-east of Truro, this attractive riverside village used to be a port and was a centre for boatbuilding. Today it is the low-water embarkation point for River Fal boat trips between Truro and Falmouth. The Truro River between the city and Malpas forms the Malpas Site of Special Scientific Interest, on account of its mudflats, wildfowl, and some fish species. Its steeply sloping banks are lined with rows of terraced cottages with stunning views of the river. It can be reached from Boscawen Park via a pretty riverside walk, passing the little beach at Sunny Corner, which takes around forty minutes. Birdwatchers will be on the lookout for waders who concentrate here if the tide is coming in. The name Malpas derives from the French and means 'dangerous crossing' since tidal currents can be unpredictable here. For at least a thousand years there was a ferry across to the opposite bank which formed a link between Truro and the estate of Tregothnan, home of the Boscawen family, on the Roseland peninsula. According to a poem by Beroul, a twelfth-century Norman writer, it was used by Iseult (heroine of the Tristan and Isolde legend) to reach King Mark's palace in the vicinity of Kea. In more recent times there was a bell at Malpas which was used to summon the ferryman or woman from their cottage on the other side. During the early nineteenth century the ferry was operated by a formidable lady known as Jenny Mopas and a painting of her by John Boyle hangs in the servants' quarters at Tregothnan House (not open to the public). She once foiled a robbery and took the felon prisoner single-handedly! When asked which passengers were most troublesome to convey in her rowing boat, named the *Happy Go Lucky*, she is said to

The Truro River at Sunny Corner near Malpas.

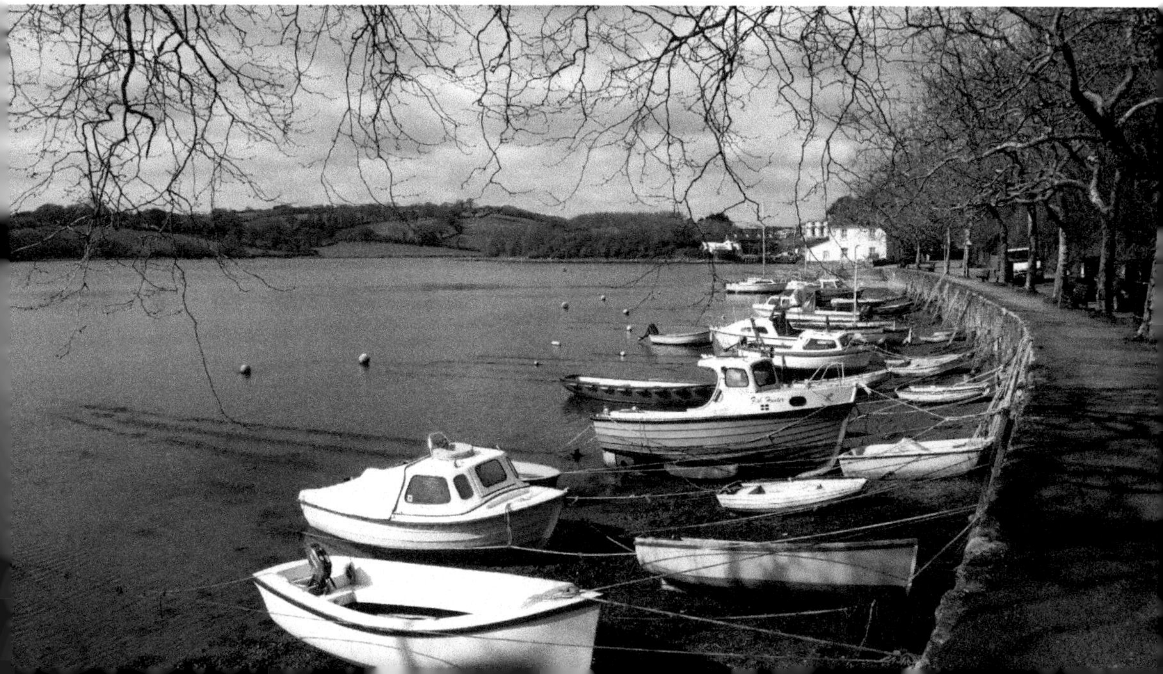

have replied 'wemmin and pigs'! A nice place to eat or enjoy a drink is the Heron Inn, which has lovely views of the tourist boats bound for Falmouth along the river that the Victorians called the Cornish Rhine.

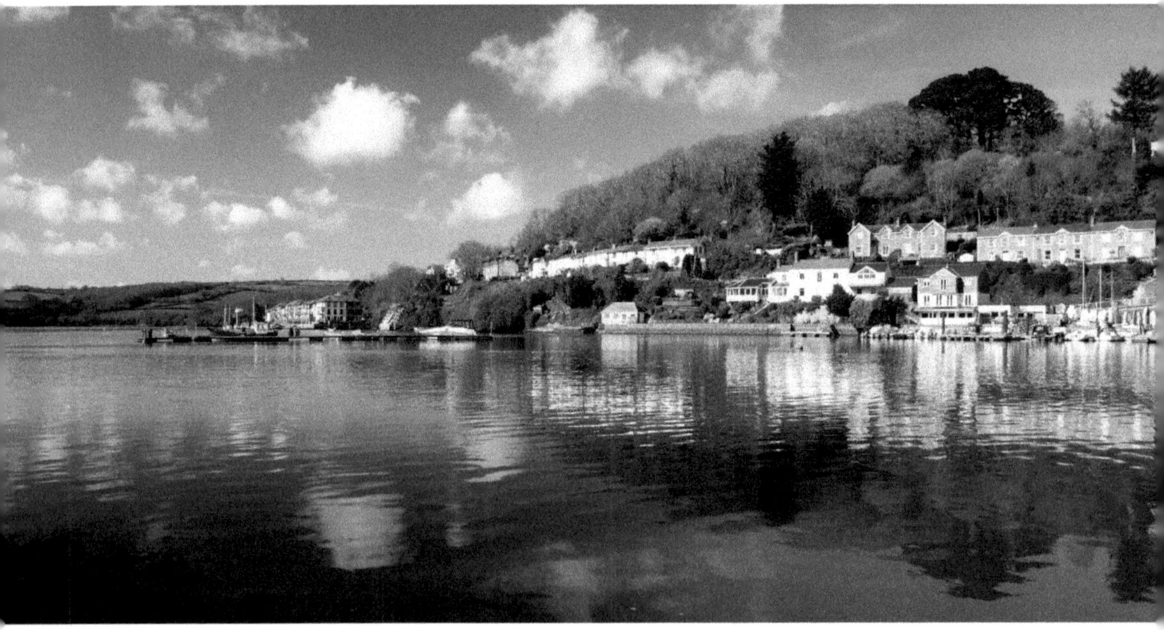

Above: Malpas seen from across the Truro River.

Below: A River Fal excursion approaches Malpas.

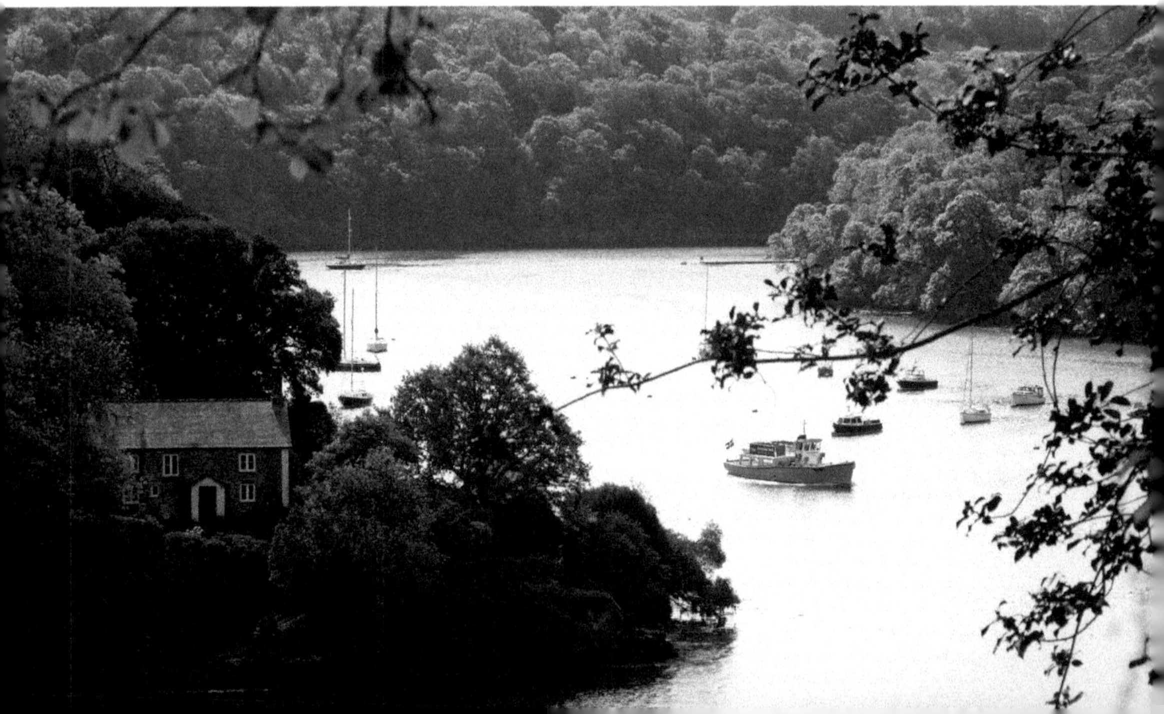

N

Newham Trail

Newham, on the western bank of the Truro River, was mentioned as long ago as 1364 as *Nyuham*. Today it is home to an industrial estate, some offices and apartments, and the Port of Truro. On the trackbed of the former Newham branch line, which was opened by the West Cornwall Railway in 1855, this 2-mile-long trail takes us from Newham Quay to Highertown in the vicinity of New County Hall. There is very little of the railway infrastructure left today, save the road bridges at Calenick and Penweathers, plus an overgrown brick-built lineside shed.

Calenick Creek seen through trees near Newham.

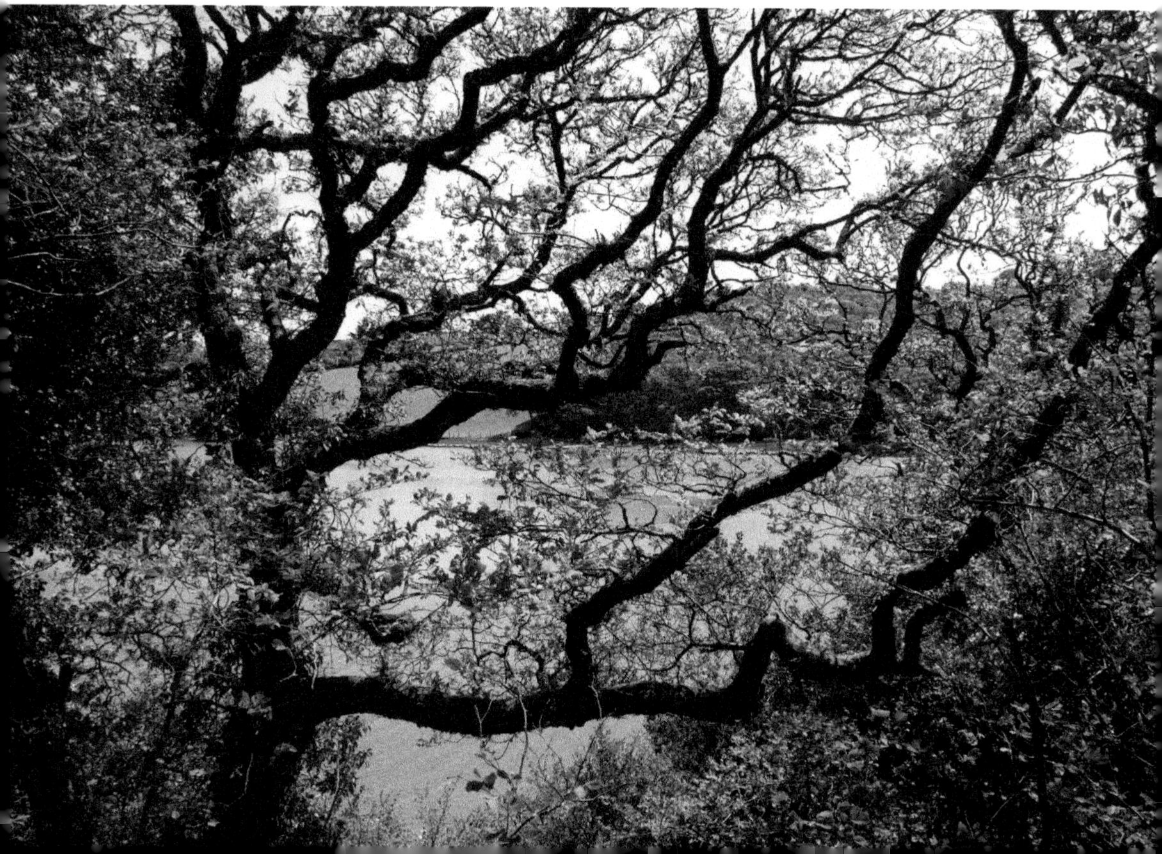

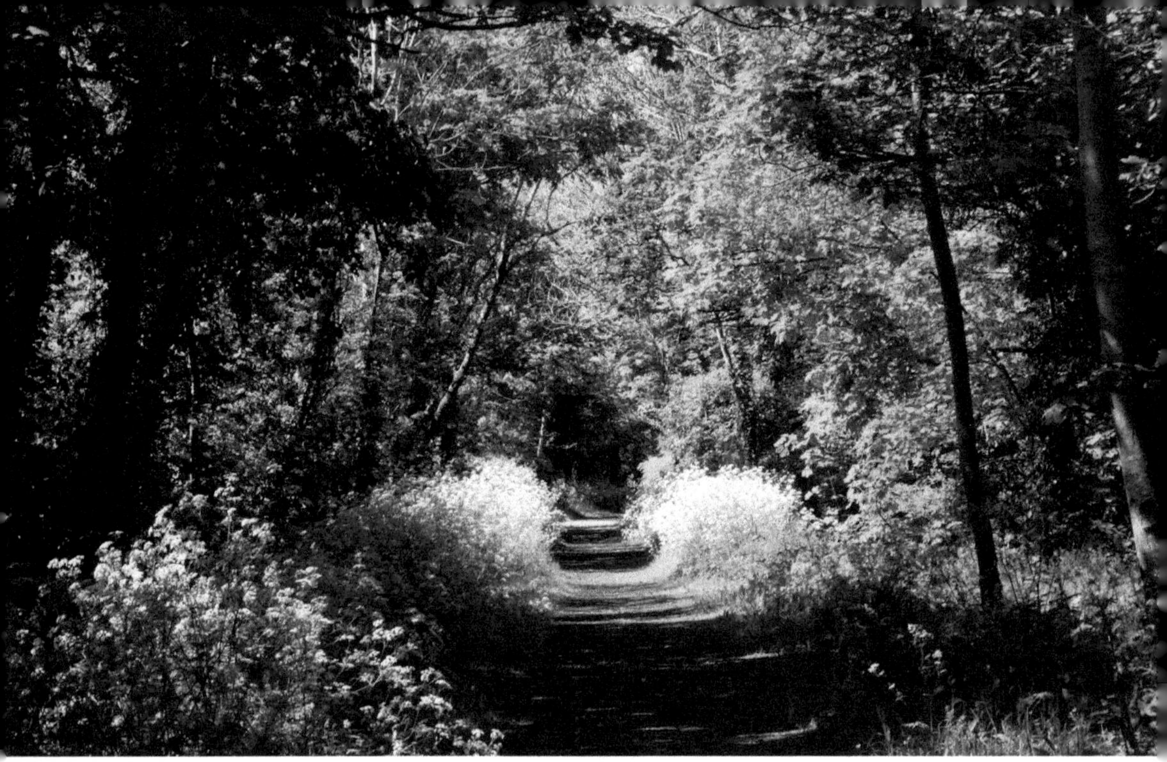

The Newham trail between Calenick and Penweathers.

The trail begins at Newham Quay at the foot of picturesquely named Gas Hill (the site of the town's former gasworks) where there is a small car park. It is often full, the nearest parking then being at the Garras Wharf car park around a ten-minute walk away. Avoid the larger car park further up Gas Hill, which is privately owned, and allow at least two hours to complete the return trip. Being a former railway, the trail is flat of course, and, once past the sheds of the industrial estate, the first section follows Calenick Creek, which joins the Truro River just downstream of the Port of Truro. It is well screened by trees apart from a few open sections where a glimpse of the countryside beyond the creek is obtained. You may be lucky enough to spot some swans or more likely hear their wing beats as they take off from the water. At the road junction it is worth making a detour to explore the hamlet of Calenick. From here, the trail continues across the main A39 Truro to Falmouth road, then makes its way up to the former junction with the Falmouth branch line at Penweathers. You can either return along the trail or make your way up to Highertown and return through the city, with extensive views of the cathedral which dominates the cityscape in front of you.

The Newham branch was the original route taken by the West Cornwall railway as it made its way east from Penzance via Redruth. Initially there was a station serving Truro at Highertown, but when the line was extended to Newham this was closed and Newham became the terminus for Truro. Not for long, however, as after the opening of the Tamar Bridge in 1859, the Cornwall railway (later the GWR) reached Truro from the east and the current mainline station, closer to the city centre, took over the role. The Newham branch continued as a goods-only line until its closure in 1965.

O

Opes

A characteristic that Truro shares with other Cornish towns are the narrow passageways which often form shortcuts between streets. Throughout the county these are known as opes (pronounced 'ops') and are often given what seem to us amusing names, frequently based on Cornish dialect. In Truro several are named after some long-gone citizens, perhaps traders or business people in the town. These include Roberts Ope, Tippet's Backlet (Tippet was the owner of a fulling mill), Coombe's Lane, Pearson's Ope, Tonkin's Ope, Swifty's Ope, Nalder's Court, Job's Court and Carne's Ope, although this last has now been blocked off by building extensions. Perhaps the most memorable is Squeeze Guts Alley (see separate entry).

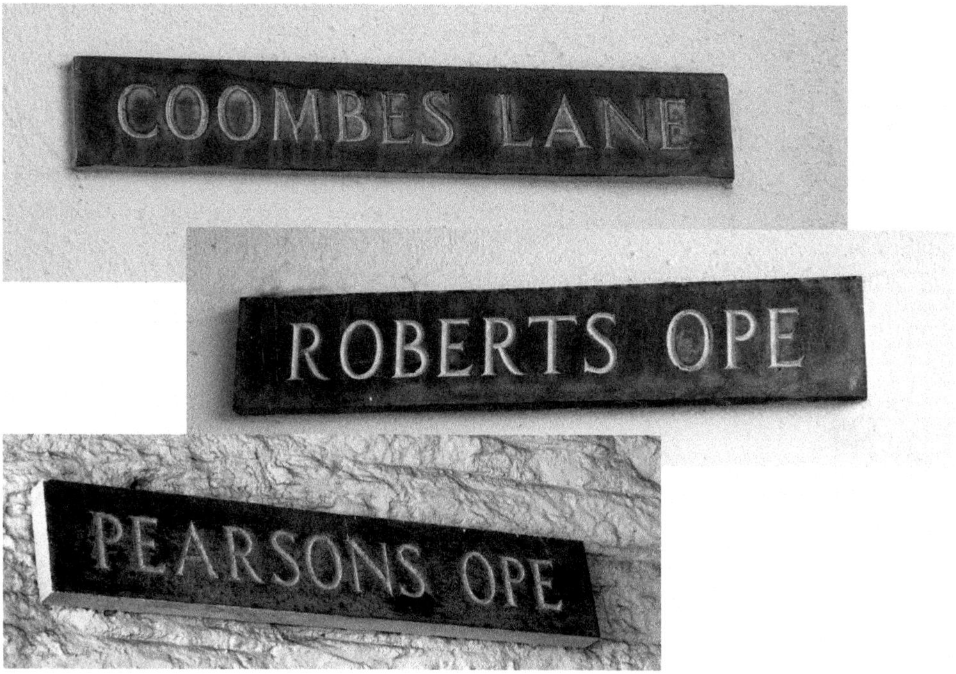

Truro's opes.

Ormond, Guillaume

Among the famous organists who have played the Father Willis organ in Truro Cathedral, one of the most memorable was Guillaume Ormond, known to all as G. O., who was born in 1896 in Italy. A nephew of artist John Singer Sargent, he was appointed by bishop Walter Frere in 1929. He held the post of organist and master of the choristers for a phenomenal forty-one years, enough time for a fund of amusing stories about his absent-mindedness to accumulate. He was particularly forgetful about his mode of transport around the county. He would drive to a town or village to practise, then forget his car and take the train home. Next morning, finding the garage empty, he would phone the police to report his car stolen. On one occasion, whilst driving, he had his mind on some tricky organ piece and started practising on the dashboard, quickly regaining control as the car veered across the road! When practising in a church at St Blazey, he dropped the organ key into the depths of the instrument. Imagine the surprise the vicar had when he looked in later to find G. O. perched high up with a fishing rod trying to retrieve the lost key from the depths of the instrument.

Ormond was described by the French organist Marcel Dupré as the greatest English organist of his time (he had taken British citizenship in 1918). He was forced to retire with ill health in 1970 and died a few months afterwards. There is a plaque to his memory near the organ.

P

Penrose, Annie 'Spitfire'

On 2 October 2011 centenarian Annie Penrose died in a Truro care home. Brought up in India during the last years of the Raj, she was the daughter of Sir Robert McLean, a railway executive. Annie was a spirited child with a fiery temper, and her father gave her the nickname of Little Spitfire. When the family returned to Britain in 1929, Sir Robert joined the board of Vickers Aviation, who were the owners of the Supermarine aircraft factory in Southampton. As chairman of the company, he worked closely with R. J. Mitchell, who was designing a new single-seater fighter plane codenamed K5054. When the time came to give the new plane a name, McLean wanted the aircraft to be called something venomous and in the tradition of the company, starting with a sibilant sound. His mind went back to his daughter's childhood nickname, and so was born the most famous fighter plane of all time. The story goes that Mitchell hated the name, preferring *Shrew*.

At around this time Annie married the actor Robert Newton but the marriage didn't last and following a divorce she went on to marry her former sister-in-law's ex-husband, Beakus Penrose, and the couple bought Killiow House near Truro. This was the project she needed, and together they developed the estate into a thriving farm and gardens. Every spring when the estate opened to the public she would sit astride her horse and blow a hunting horn. To celebrate her 100th birthday, a flypast took place at Falmouth towing a banner bearing the greeting 'Happy 100th Birthday Spitfire Annie'. Truro has another connection with the Spitfire, for during the Second World War wing parts for the plane underwent repair in the H. T. P. workshop on Lemon Quay, on the site of the present Pannier Market.

Percy, Thomas Bickle

Truro's manufacturing chemist, Thomas Percy M. P. S., claimed to be the world's leading manufacturer of rennet. Extracted from the fourth stomach of nursing calves, rennet was used in the making of cheese and the much-loved Westcountry dessert junket. Thomas was born in Launceston and grew up in Tavistock, where his father was an innkeeper. In 1864 he married his first wife, Henrietta Rich, in Somerset. After she died in 1871, he remarried two years later, to Philippa Hitchens, the daughter of a shipping agent. In 1888 she also died, and he married for the third time in 1897. He was described as a man of retiring disposition, who had a lucrative sideline as a lessee of tolls and market and harbour dues throughout Cornwall, including the Torpoint Ferry. Leasing the right to collect tolls and dues was a family business, with members of the Percy family recorded as toll collectors as far afield as Somerset, Hammersmith and Carmarthenshire.

Thomas Percy began making his Double Strength Essence of Rennet in 1862 and he boasted that it had won over sixty awards and was used to make the junket consumed at the Great Devonian Dinners held annually in London. We do not know where he learnt his trade, but he spent some time in Bridgwater as a toll collector prior to starting his business in Truro, and may well have observed the use of rennet in cheesemaking whilst there. His potions were made at the family home in Victoria Place, which he named Medical Hall, with the help of an assistant, William Patridge, who later went on to become a fully fledged pharmacist and dentist in Liverpool. Since he was already established before the Pharmacy Act of 1868, Percy was able to register as a chemist and druggist without an examination. In the late 1880s, trade directories gave his address as No. 11 River Street.

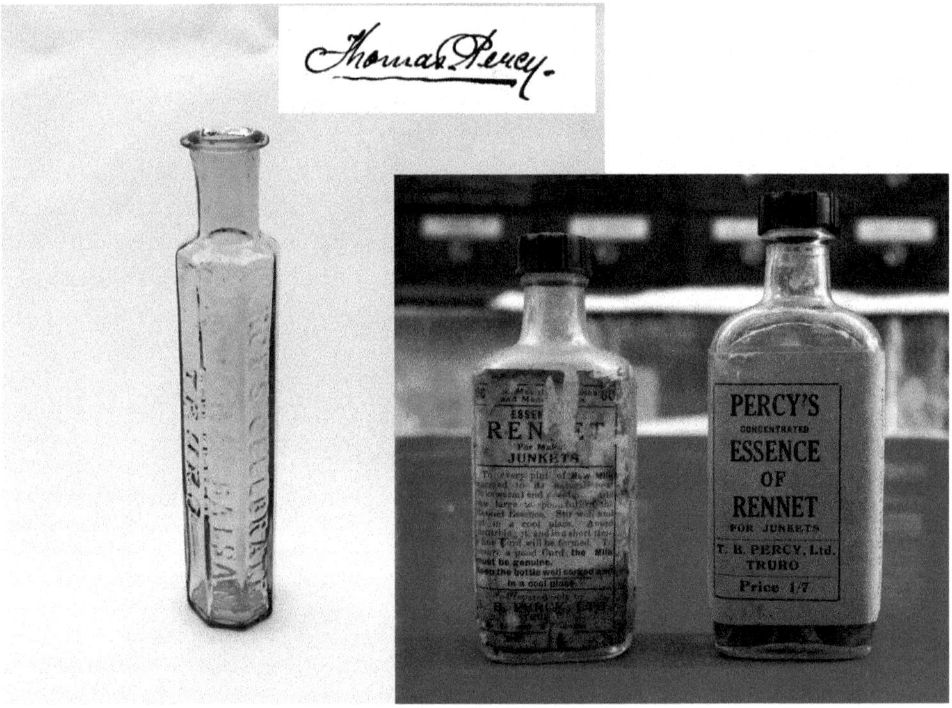

(*Left*) a blue glass Percy's Pectoral Balsam bottle (photo courtesy of Amanda Hawkins, Showpiece Antiques), and (*right*) Percy's Rennet bottles. (*Inset*) Thomas Percy's signature.

In common with many chemists supplying over-the-counter remedies in Victorian times, Percy advertised his wares using testimonials from satisfied customers, especially well-known show business or aristocratic names. His rennet was praised by the Dowager Lady Bowring and his Pectoral Balsam was endorsed by music hall comic James Fawn, who declared that it was the best patent medicine he had ever tasted. It was sold in an elegant octagonal blue-glass bottle and Mr Percy claimed that it would cure coughs, colds, shortness of breath, asthma, spitting of blood, bronchitis, influenza, spasms, pains in the chest and consumption. He also had overseas customers, the aristocratic-sounding Duc de Montabor apparently writing from France to praise his Balsam of Aniseed, which he claimed had completely restored his health. Another best-seller was dandelion coffee, extracted from dandelion root and recommended for weak digestion, nervous and dyspeptic affections, and flatulence. Thomas Percy died in 1921 at the age of eighty-four in Plymouth, where he had business interests in property companies. His son James took over his rennet business, which continued until the 1970s.

Potts, Dr Lawrence Holker

Dr Potts has been described as one of the keenest of brains that ever practised in Cornwall. Not just a physician, he was also a scientist and engineer. In 1812, at the age of only twenty-two, he was appointed as medical officer to the Devon and Cornwall Miner's Militia, who at the time were serving in Ireland. When the unit returned to Truro in 1814, he came with them and started a practice in the town. He stayed until 1838, when he moved to Blackheath. In 1821 strange happenings in Carclew Street, where the militia had their armoury, came to his notice. The household of Sergeant Ashburn of the militia began to experience curious incidents which were widely attributed to supernatural causes. Windows were broken by stones, the origin of which could not be traced. The attacks continued for ten days, and despite windows being boarded up, stones still managed to break cups and plates inside. The strain led to Sergeant Ashburn falling ill, and Dr Potts was summoned. Potts knew the family well and began to suspect that one of the Ashburns' older children, Tom, might be the perpetrator. He had been brought up by his grandmother in Lancashire, where he had worked as child labour in a cotton mill. Potts had arranged for Tom to return to Truro, where he believed he would have a better upbringing, arriving in the Ashburn household in 1819. Since then he had been subject to strict discipline from the Ashburns, and it appeared he resented this. When the stones started to fly again a week or two later, Tom was accused of the crime and suffered a fit, losing consciousness. Potts examined him and by the simple subterfuge of calling loudly for a horse-whip, concluded that the boy was feigning unconsciousness, observing a quickening of his pulse rate at the mention of the whip. The boy made a full confession and calm returned to the Ashburn household.

As well as his medical work, Potts' inventive mind was coming up with ideas for mechanical devices. One of his more hare-brained schemes, which he patented in 1843, was to transport letters by suspending them on wires hung between church towers! His most successful invention involved the use of air pressure to sink tubes into soft sand, for which he obtained a patent in 1843. A prototype device was tested on the Goodwin Sands, where it was successfully used to sink the foundations for a beacon tower. A number of railway viaducts were also built with the technology, including sinking nineteen tubes across an estuary on the island of Anglesey in 1846. His invention eventually absorbed most of his money, as he spent the last years of his life trying to perfect it. His knowledge of science also led him to become one of the founders and the first secretary of the Royal Institution of Cornwall in 1818.

Princes Street

In terms of the quality of its architecture, Princes Street is considered to be second only to Lemon Street, but its north-facing aspect deprives its impressive façades of the best light. It contains two fine town houses designed by Thomas Edwards. Princes House dates from 1740 and was built for mining magnate William Lemon. It was complete with its own chapel (and organ), and its grounds went as far as the quay, and

Princes House, Princes Street.

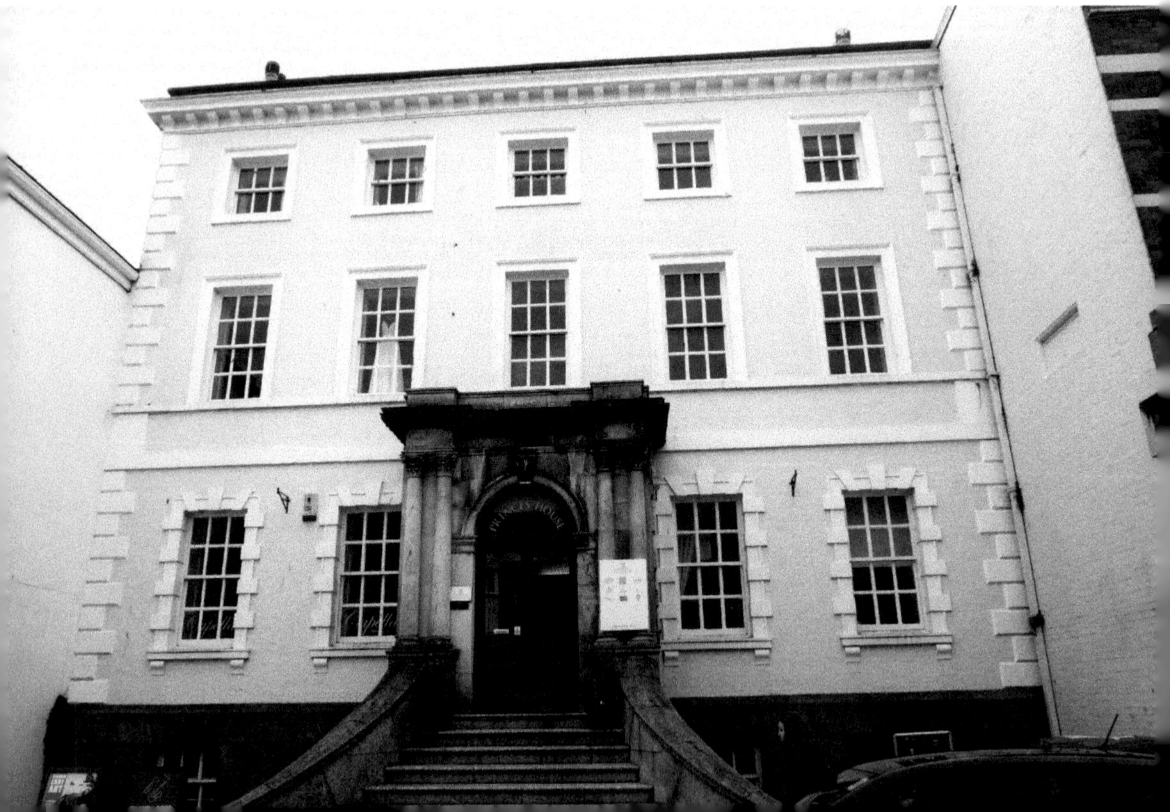

are now occupied by the Pannier Market. The Mansion House was built for Lemon's one-time clerk, Thomas 'Guinea a Minute' Daniell (see separate entry), between 1755 and 1762 and faced with Bath stone supplied by Ralph Allen, who was Daniell's uncle by marriage. The rococo-style decoration in the living room and staircase are said to have been the work of French prisoners of war.

As well as the development of Bath stone as a building material, Ralph Allen is also famous for his reforms of the postal service. A Cornishman, Allen became the Postmaster of Bath at the age of only nineteen, and as his career progressed, he went on to introduce many practices which increased the efficiency of the postal system. Allen died in 1764, almost a century before the introduction of the postbox, but it is fitting that across the street from the Mansion House is an example of postal history, an early Penfold pillar box dating from the 1860s.

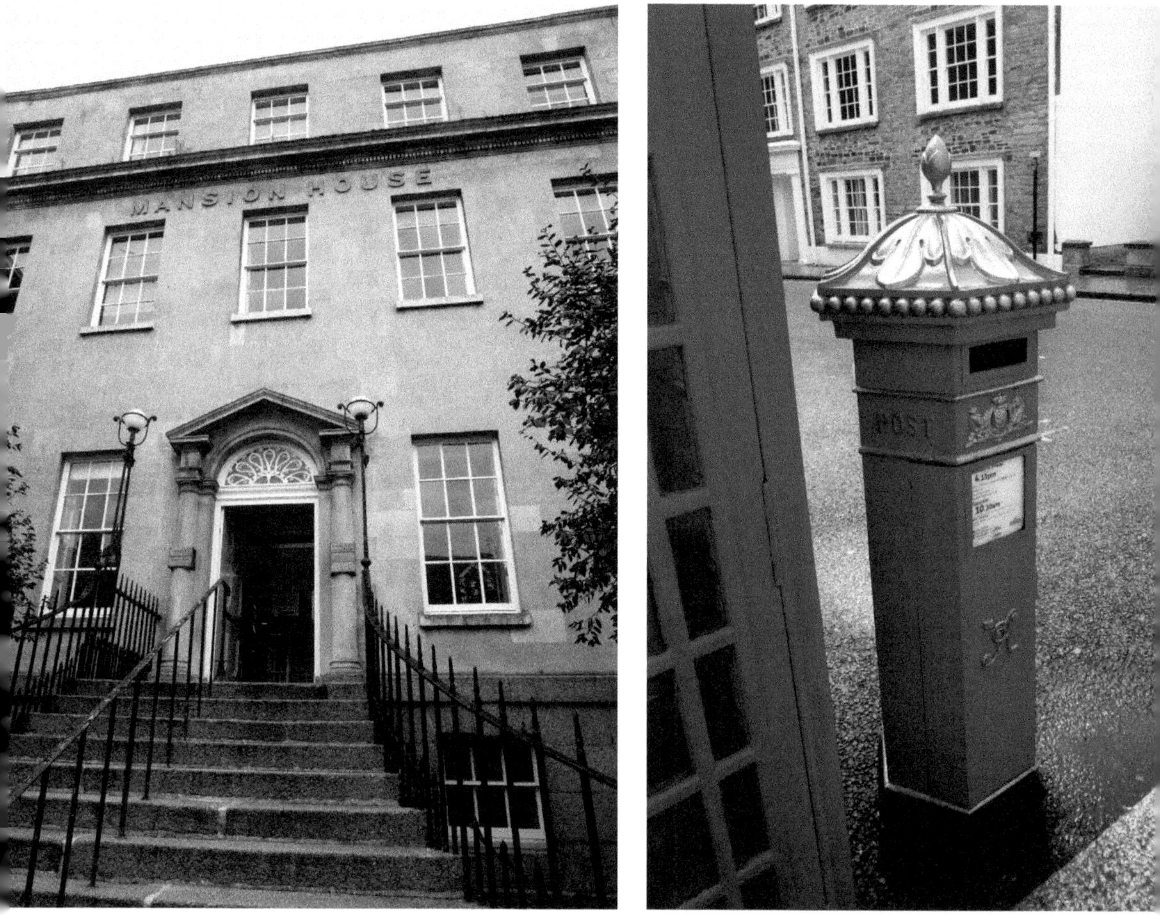

Princes Street: Mansion House (*left*) and Penfold pillar box (*right*).

Q

Queen

On 27 June 1970, Truro's City Hall had been booked for a gig by a London band, *Smile*. The band's drummer, Roger Taylor, had grown up in Truro and the appearance was arranged by his mother to raise money for charity. It turned out to be an important night in rock music history.

Born in Norfolk, Roger's family moved to Truro in 1957, and he joined the cathedral choir two years later. After leaving school, Roger, who had played the drums in local bands, went up to London to study dentistry at Imperial College. On the student union noticeboard he saw an advertisement for a drummer, placed there by an astrophysics student called Brian May. The band was called *Smile* and May was the guitarist, along with a singer called Tim Stafell. Roger joined the band and they visited Cornwall on an almost monthly basis, sometimes staying in Truro in Roger's mum's bungalow. On occasions a certain Freddie Bulsara came with them and eventually replaced Tim, making his debut as their vocalist in Truro on that June evening. One further last-minute change was made that night: to reflect the change in line-up, the band was renamed *Queen*. Their first public performance was on stage in Truro with the soon-to-be Freddie Mercury as vocalist, and the band's fee for performing that night was the princely sum of £50! Subsequently they made regular appearances in the city at PJ's nightclub in Pydar Street. Roger also wrote many of the band's hits, including '*Radio Gaga*' and '*A Kind of Magic*'. In 1999 he became the first living person apart from members of the royal family to appear on a British stamp, rather in the background to the late Freddie Mercury it must be admitted. In 2011 he returned in the city to unveil the Drummer Statue on Lemon Quay.

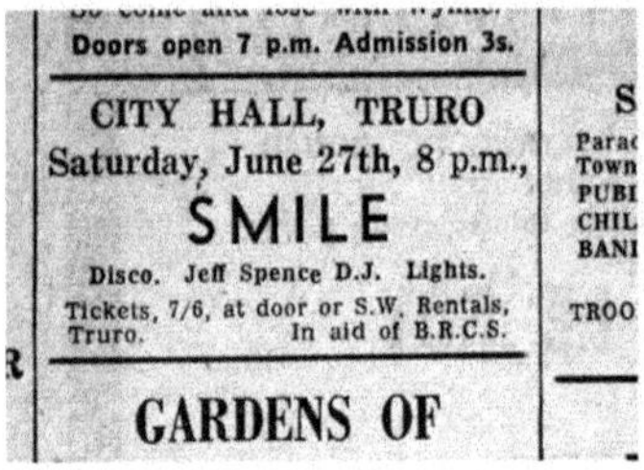
Doors open 7 p.m. Admission 3s.
CITY HALL, TRURO
Saturday, June 27th, 8 p.m.,
SMILE
Disco. Jeff Spence D.J. Lights.
Tickets, 7/6, at door or S.W. Rentals, Truro. In aid of B.R.C.S.
GARDENS OF

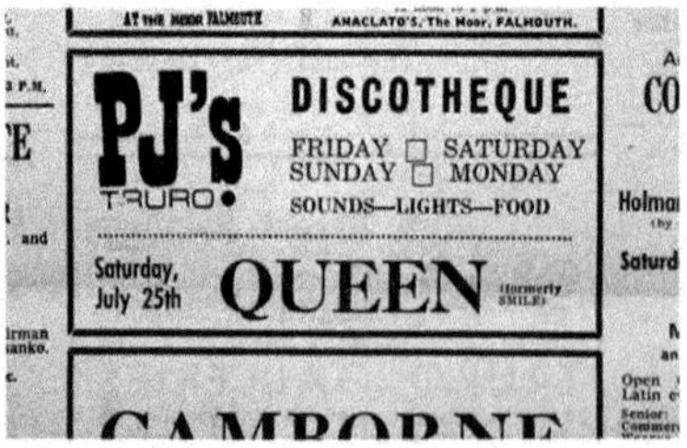
ANACLATO'S, The Moor, FALMOUTH.
PJ's TRURO
DISCOTHEQUE
FRIDAY SATURDAY SUNDAY MONDAY
SOUNDS—LIGHTS—FOOD
Saturday, July 25th
QUEEN (formerly SMILE)

Newspaper advertisements for *Queen's* debut performances in Truro. (Courtesy of Rupert White)

R

Roundabout of the Year

Not content with winning prizes for the city's parks, the municipal gardeners of Truro have also won a national award for the best roundabout in Britain! In the summer of 2019, the Trafalgar roundabout became the home of four giant hedgehogs, made locally from coppiced wood. Cecil, Denzil, Kizzy and Patricia moved into their new home in the middle of a traffic island helped by humans from Wild Truro and Truro City Parks Department. Since then they have been featured on breakfast television and the Chris Evan's radio show, which led to the roundabout receiving the prestigious Roundabout of the Year award from the Roundabout Appreciation Society! They also featured on the cover and December page of the society's 2020 calendar. To encourage garden owners to look after hedgehogs, Cecil and his friends have even been covered with piles of sticks for the winter.

The Trafalgar Roundabout, named Roundabout of the Year 2020.

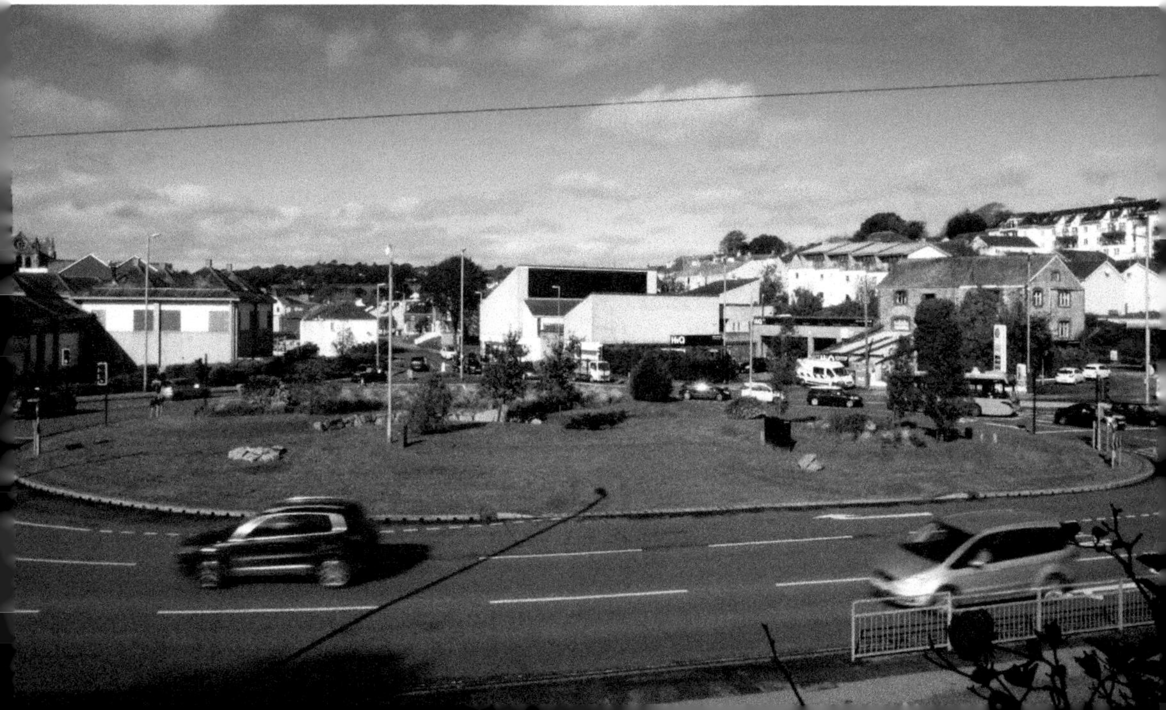

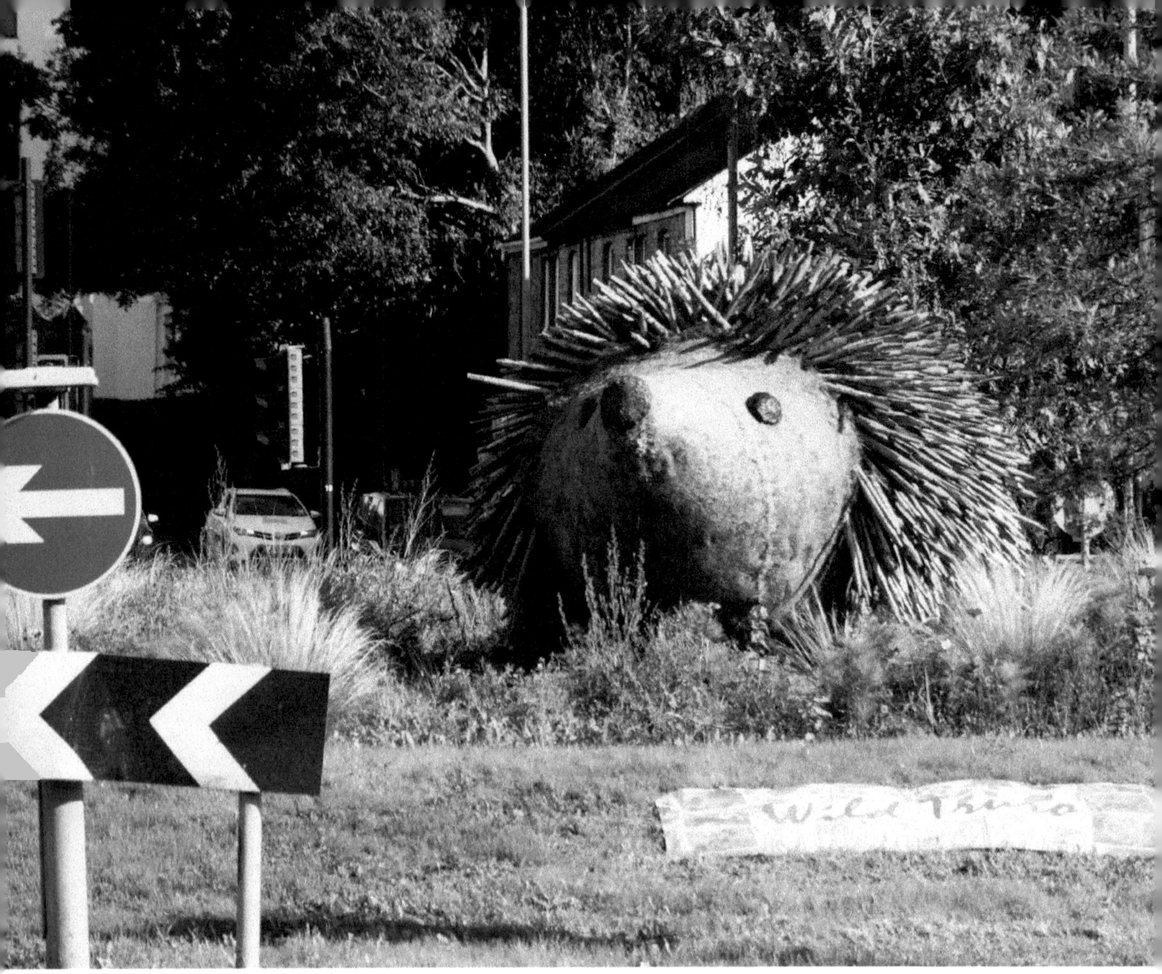

One of the Trafalgar Roundabout hedgehogs.

Royal Cornwall Museum

In the early nineteenth century Cornwall had become the centre of mining technology and was famous for its innovations in engineering, ranging from the use of steam power to the sinking of shafts and refining of ore. The presence of so much knowledge in the area led to the founding of the Cornwall Literary and Philosophical Institution in 1818. Its brief was the promotion of knowledge in natural history, archaeology, ethnology and the fine and industrial arts, especially in relation to Cornwall. It became the Royal Institution of Cornwall in 1821. There were plenty of rich patrons living in Truro, and the first museum was opened in Union Place in a building that was formerly the home of the Vivian family. In 1919 it moved to the newly acquired Truro Savings Bank building in River Street (see Philip Sambell) and in 1998 expanded into the adjoining former Baptist church building, designed by the same architect.

Today the museum has displays of Ancient Greek, Roman and Egyptian artefacts supported by the British Museum, a ceramics collection on loan from the V and A, and the collection of Cornish minerals once belonging to Philip Rashleigh of Menabilly,

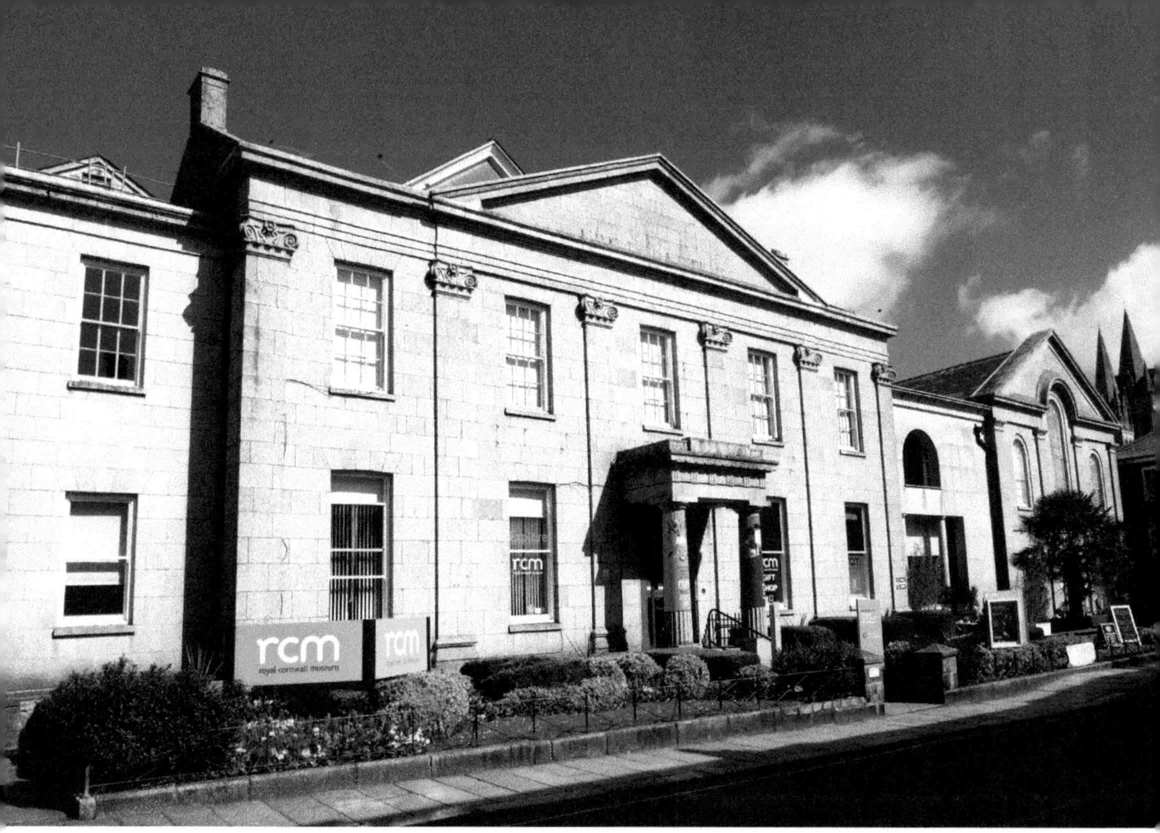

The Royal Cornwall Museum building in River Street includes the former Baptist church.

which Thomas Keam helped to curate. In its fine art collection are examples of work by enameller Henry Bone, sculptor Neville Northey Burnard, and painter John Opie, all famous Cornishmen. It also houses the Courtney library, one of the most significant collections of manuscripts relating to Cornish history. It holds 40,000 books, pamphlets and other printed matter, including the correspondence of steam pioneer Richard Trevithick and a collection of original manuscripts by Poldark author Winston Graham.

At the time of writing it is planned to close the museum for the first eight months of 2020. This is partly to carry out roof repairs, but the underlying issue seems to be falling visitor numbers. The press release tells us that the museum that reopens in September 2020 'will be different, following a consultation to understand and meet the changing needs of visitors and to sustain the service for the future'.

S

Sambell, Philip

Even by the standards of today's equal opportunities society, it is remarkable that a deaf-mute child born in 1798 in Devonport should be educated well enough to have a successful career as an architect. The eldest of ten children, Philip Sambell came to Truro in 1822 with his family after his father, Philip Snr, who owned a successful shipping business, found himself bankrupt after the theft of one of his ships and her cargo. In Truro, he set up a timber business based at Lemon Quay, which soon proved profitable. By this time, it appears that Philip Jnr was already following his chosen career as an architect. Our knowledge of his early life and education is very scant as most of the school records from the time were destroyed in the Plymouth Blitz. In his later writings he told of a voyage to Ireland where he had a conversation 'on the fingers' with a fellow passenger, showing that he had learned sign language. It is not known how he trained as an architect, but this must have taken place before the family left Plymouth, and he was probably influenced by John Foulston, who had moved from London to Devonport where he had designed a number of important public buildings. Philip Jnr's written work reveals a keen and intelligent brain; he was a skilled surveyor and his drawings were meticulous. He even gave lectures

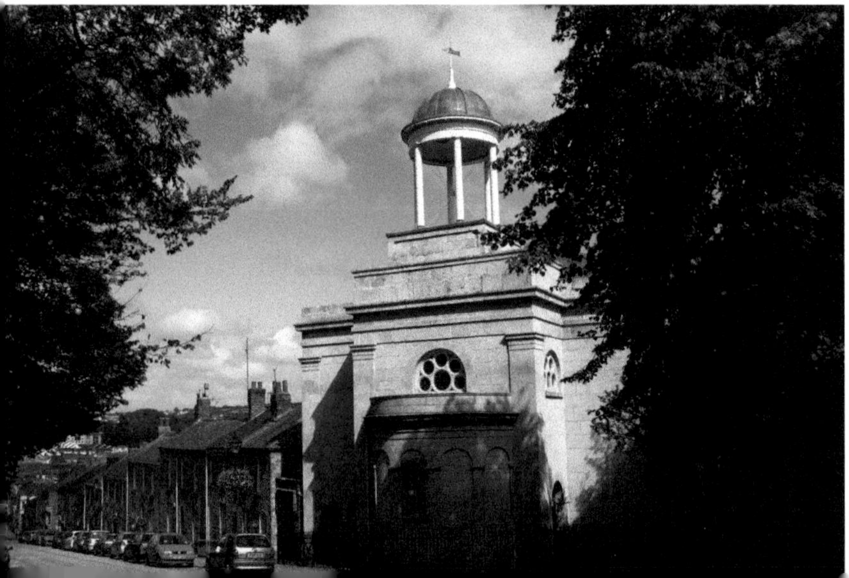

St John's Church, Lemon Street, designed by Philip Sambell.

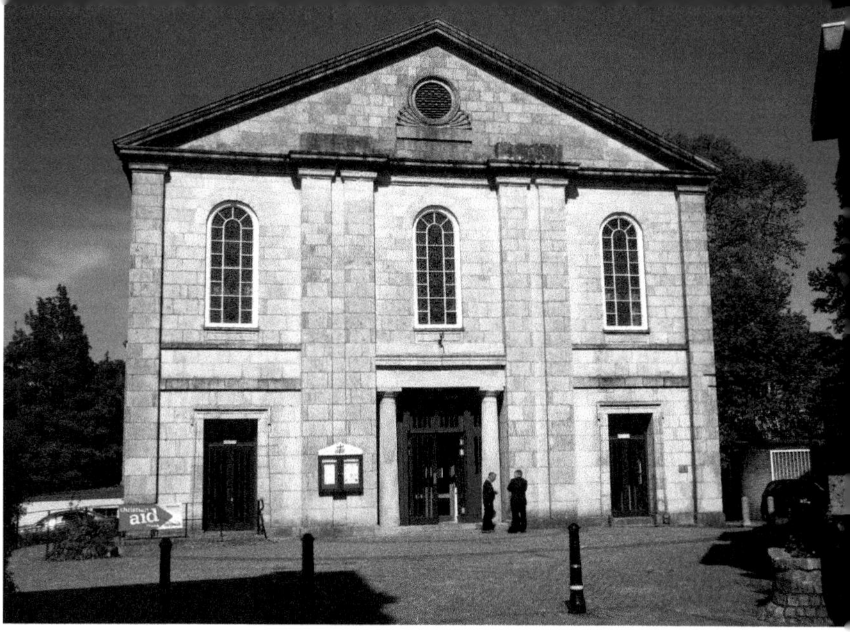

St Mary Clement Methodist church, Union Place, designed by Philip Sambell.

throughout his career, read by an assistant, on topics as wide ranging as science, engineering and religion as well as his chosen profession.

Philip's first commission was for the church of St John's at the top of Lemon Street, the foundation stone of which was laid with much ceremony in 1827. He had designed a church in the Italianate style with a pillared cupola bell tower on the roof, an unusual style for a Cornish town, and possibly inspired by St John's Church in Devonport. There followed numerous commissions for nonconformist chapels and churches throughout the county, including Truro Baptist church in River Street (of which he would later become a deacon), now part of the Royal Cornwall Museum, and St Mary's Methodist church in Union Place. He disliked the elaborate Gothic-style beloved of Anglican churches, preferring classical lines. Oddly in view of his disability, his chapels were designed with the acoustics in mind, limiting the floor area and building galleries to accommodate larger congregations.

In the 1820s Philip met local property developer Josephus Ferris, who had been buying up agricultural land on the edge of the old town on which to build houses. This was along the Kenwyn valley in the area of what has now become Frances Street, Castle Street and Edward Street, an area later dubbed Ferris Town. Philip was commissioned to design villas to appeal to the merchants and businessmen of the expanding town. In Castle Street, Castle Lodge and Castle Villa are particularly fine examples of his style. He also designed Georgian town houses along Strangways Terrace leading off Lemon Street on land owned by Sir Charles Lemon. In 1837 it is thought that he designed Walsingham Place (see separate entry).

In 1834 disaster struck the Sambell family when Philip Snr was declared bankrupt for a second time, and spent a short time in prison. After the sale of all his assets, the family retired to live in the nearby village of St Clements. In the same year Philip Jnr submitted his successful design for the Lander monument in Lemon Street (see separate entry). Inspiration for this Doric column may have come from John Foulston's design for a taller column in Devonport, built in 1824.

Perhaps Philip Jnr's best-known commission was for Truro Savings Bank in River Street, adjoining the Baptist church. It opened for business in 1847, no doubt its fine classical façade with a doorway framed by Doric pillars creating the solid impression required by the bank's trustees. By 1874, however, the bank was in financial difficulties and by 1897 the building was up for sale. It was purchased by the Henderson School of Mining but in turn this institution folded in 1908. The building was eventually purchased by its present owners, the Royal Institution of Cornwall, who extended the space at the rear to create a gallery and opened the current museum in 1919.

Philip Sambell died on 5 December 1874 in Stonehouse, Plymouth. He is buried in Ford Park cemetery in the city.

Setts

Setts are the granite blocks which have long given character to Boscawen Street. Misguidedly referred to as cobbles, they are rectangular, not round, and were all hand cut from local granite. The distinctive surface is a feature of the street, which was widened in the 1790s by demolishing the middle row of shops. In 1882 the Kit Hill Granite Company supplied setts which were laid in Lower Lemon Street and King Street, both of which lead into Boscawen Street. In 2018 Cornwall's highways department decided that the setts had started to become loose, leading to the uneven surface becoming unsafe. They were removed amid a storm of local objections and stored away until a more stable surface could be created. In 2019 council workmen returned to reinstate the setts and restore the traditional appearance to Boscawen Street.

Granite setts being re-laid in Boscawen Street.

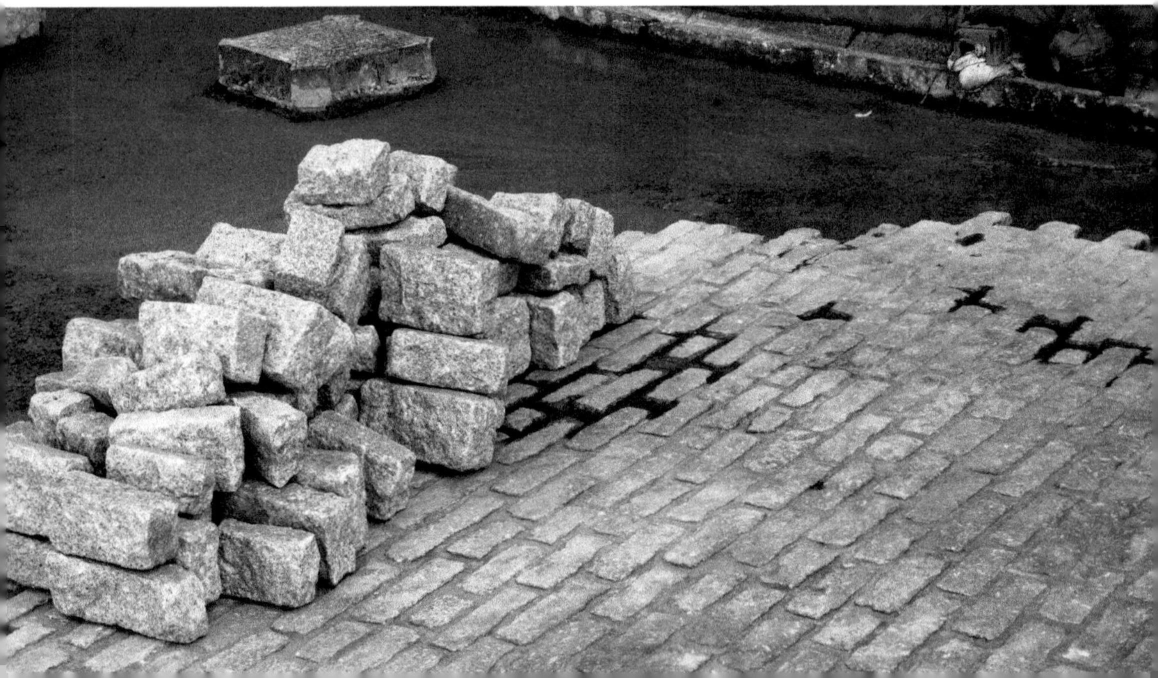

Squeeze Guts Alley

We have already mentioned Truro's characteristic opes – narrow passages linking wider streets. Undoubtedly one of the narrowest, and the most graphically named, is Squeeze Guts Alley, linking Duke Street at the eastern end of Boscawen Street with St Mary's Street behind. Once known as Duke Street Passage, it brings us out just in front of the old Grammar School building, dating from the early eighteenth century. It would have proved a useful shortcut for Cornelius Cardew, headmaster between 1771 and 1804, who was also mayor, since the council offices were across Boscawen Street.

Whilst the most likely origin of the name is the obvious one, it has also been suggested that it might stem from the days when the alley adjoined a fish market, and the guts referred to were of the fishy rather than human variety. It is also haunted, at least according to the following rhyme, which was discovered by Pete Clark in a long-out-of-print book entitled *The Ghosts of Truro.* It goes:

> If, on a fine midwinter's eve,
> Through Squeezeguts Alley you should stray,
> Please beware of fiery Steve
> Who haunts this ope upon that day.

This refers to Stephen Treffry, who died in the alley on midwinter's eve in 1787. He lived in a first-floor room above the passage and, in those days before council noise-abatement officers, was in the habit of throwing hot coals onto noisy revellers who disturbed his sleep on their way home. He had in fact spent time in the borough lock-up for so doing. On that fateful night he spilled the hot coals onto his nightclothes and caught them alight. In his attempts to dowse the flames, he fell from the window onto the street below and, despite the efforts of passers-by, could not be revived.

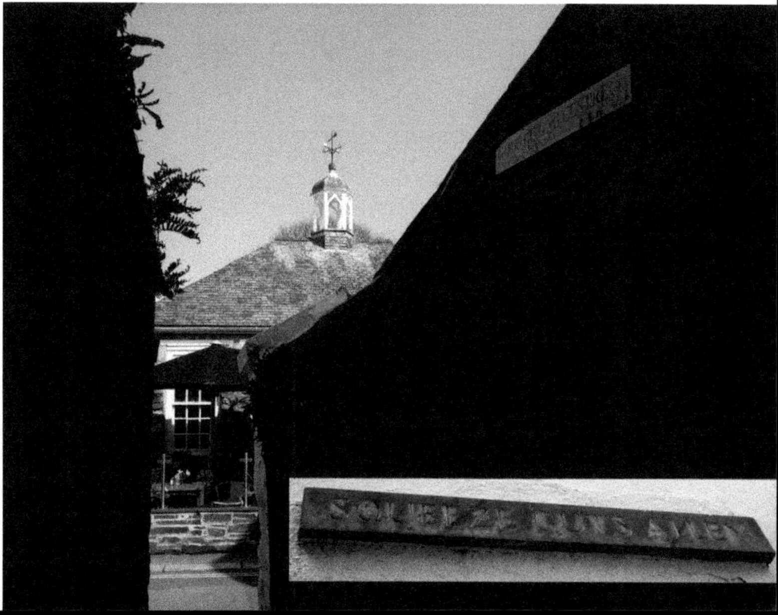

Squeeze Guts Alley.

T

Trafalgar Way

Todays instant communications mean that we can receive news of an event on the other side of the globe as it happens. In the nineteenth century news took much longer to arrive from overseas, as a plaque on the end wall of No. 81 Lemon Street demonstrates. On 21 October 1805 the Royal Navy defeated the French in the Battle of Trafalgar, the most famous casualty being, of course, Vice Admiral Lord Nelson. In order to get the news of his victory back to London, quite a relay was set up. First a fast schooner, the *Pickle*, commanded by Lt John Lapenotiere, sped from Cape Finisterre to Falmouth, arriving on 4 November. From Falmouth, Lapenotiere boarded a post-chaise and set off to cover the 371 miles to London in a dash which took thirty-seven hours with twenty-one changes of horses, the first of which took place in Truro. The news was received in London on 6 November, fifteen days after Nelson's victory.

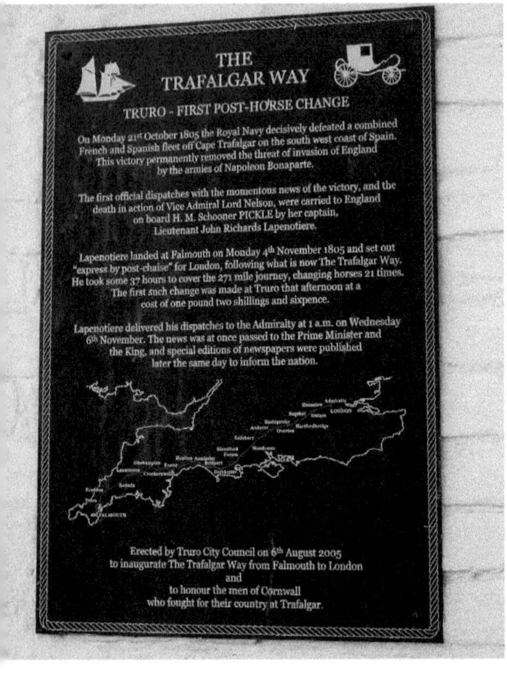

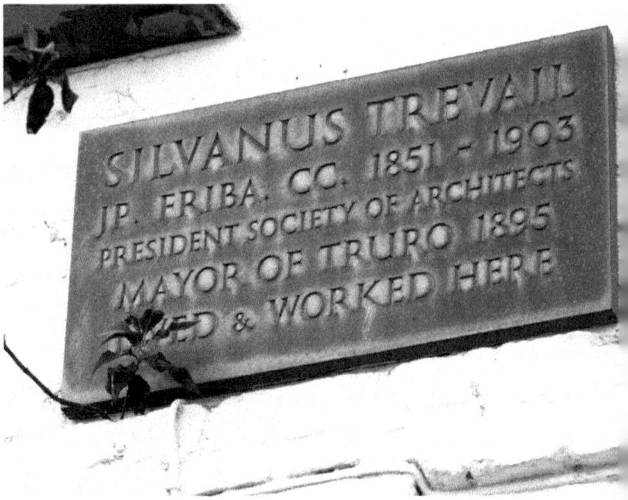

(*Left*) Trafalgar Way plaque and (*above*) plaque commemorating Sylvanus Trevail, both attached to No. 81 Lemon Street.

Trevail, Sylvanus

Higher up the end wall of No. 81 Lemon Street is a slate plaque telling us that this was the site of the offices of architect Sylvanus Trevail, one of the most prolific the county has ever produced. Born in 1851 near Luxulyan, in his lifetime he designed or renovated thirty-five churches and chapels, 100 dwellings, thirty-six commercial premises, eighteen hotels, sixteen libraries and seven hospitals, mostly in Cornwall. Of these, thirty-five were in Truro.

After leaving school in 1868, he moved to London and trained for three years, working in the Holborn offices of architect Henry Garling, who had won a competition to design the Foreign Office a few years earlier. When he returned to Cornwall, he set up an office at Par, not far from his place of birth, where he began his architectural practice. He quickly took advantage of the 1870 Education Act, which decreed that a school should be built within reach of every child, and designed most of the Victorian schools built in Cornwall as a result. In 1880 he moved his office to Truro, designing five triumphal arches for the visit of the Prince of Wales to lay the foundation stone for the cathedral. Such was his growing reputation that in 1882 he was invited to the White House and met President Arthur. He was also active

Passmore Edwards library, Pydar Street, designed by Sylvanus Trevail.

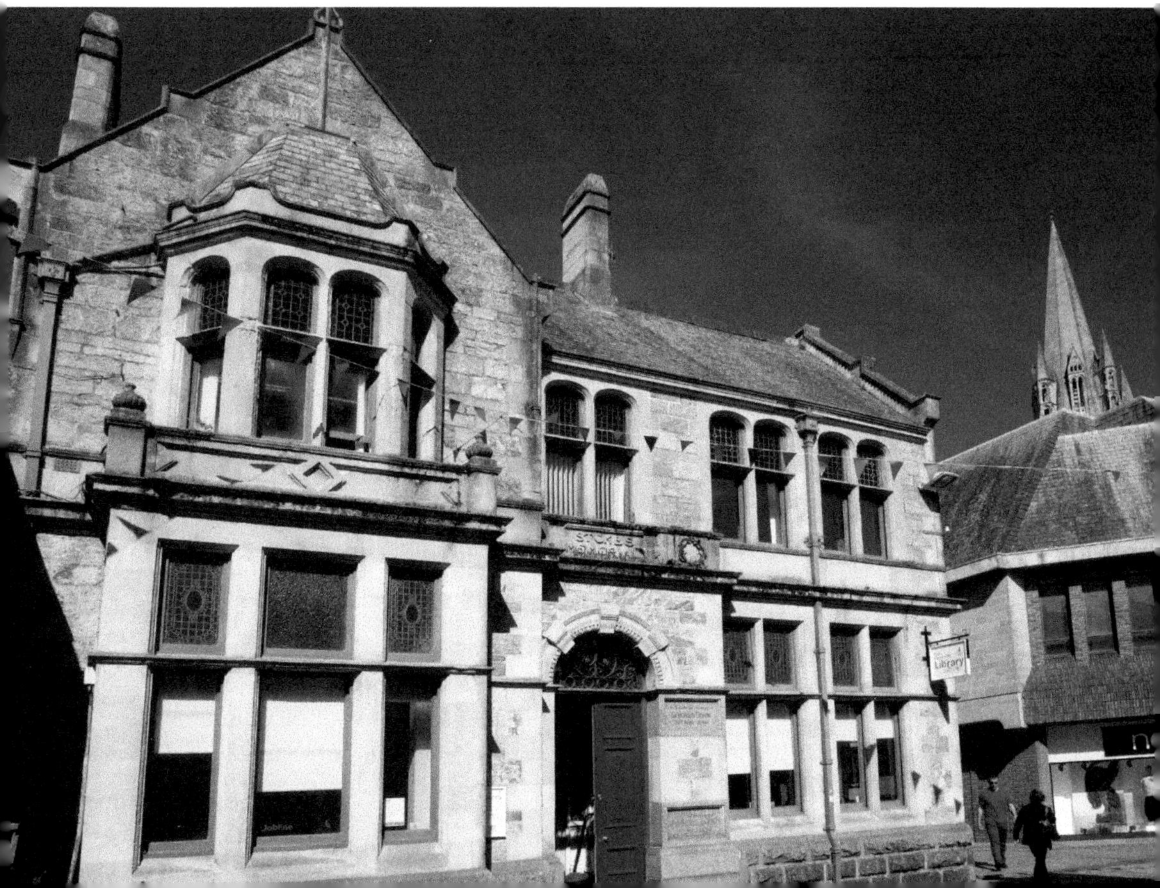

in local government and in 1894 became the 765th mayor of Truro. That same year he designed the Passmore Edwards Library in Truro's Pydar Street, still the home of the library today. Not everyone was a fan of his work: Pevsner described the Red Lion Hotel as 'terribly treated' by Trevail. Nonetheless, he was a leading figure in his profession and in 1901 became the president of the Society of Architects. His drive for success hid a secret however, as he suffered from depression. On 7 November 1903, the day of his uncle's funeral, he left his Lemon Street office and headed for Truro station where he caught the 11.40 a. m. train to London. He did not buy a first-class ticket as was his habit, opting instead for third class. At 12.40, just up the line at Par where he had opened his first office, he went into the ladies' toilet (where there was a mirror), locked the door and shot himself. The coroner concluded that business worries had unhinged his mind.

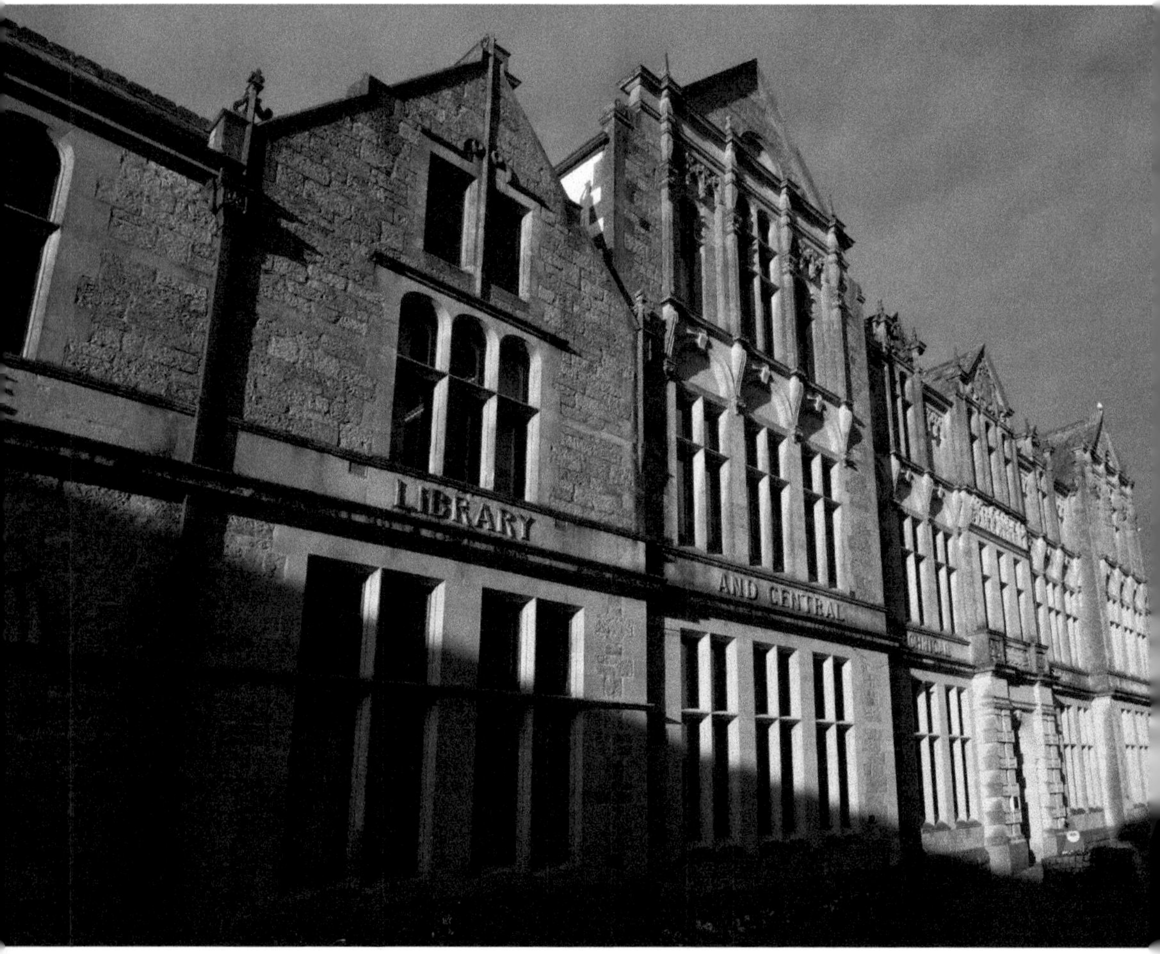

Technical School, Union Place, designed by Sylvanus Trevail.

U

Urinal

Nicknamed the *Tardis*, and with a floor area of only 44 square feet, Truro's smallest urinal stands beside Wilkes Walk above the River Allen, into which it once discharged. It was built in 1887 during the construction of the cathedral, in the grounds of which it stands. It may have been for the convenience of the workmen, or, more likely, visiting dignitaries. It is also reputed to have been used as a comfort stop by stagecoach drivers. Originally it was open to the heavens to provide the simplest form of flushing, but was roofed over at some point. In more recent years it has had several uses, including as a police box, which makes its nickname even more appropriate. It housed a police telephone before the days of radios, and still has its police lamp attached. In 2008 an estate agent placed it on the market for £19,950. Since then it has been used as an office, but its most bizarre role was in 2011 when it housed an artwork called *The lights going on and off* by Turner prize-winning artist Martin Creed.

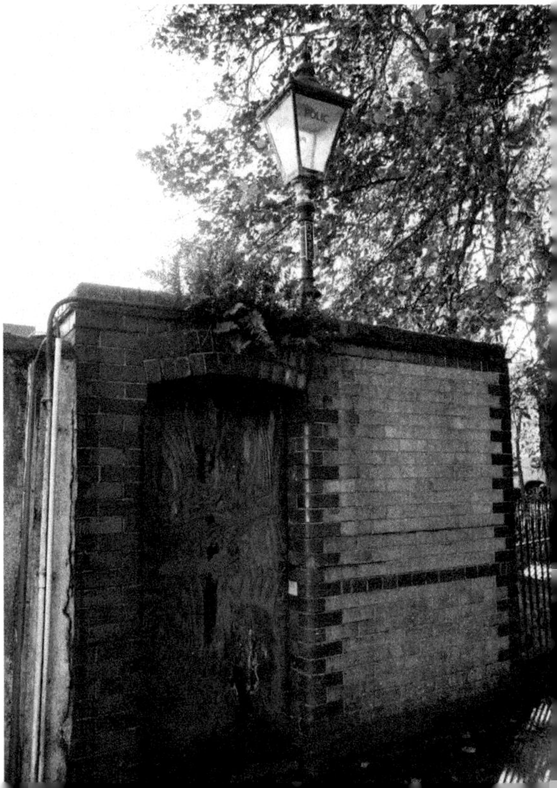

The Tardis urinal near Wilkes Walk.

V

Viaducts

The city is spanned by two viaducts: the Carvedras viaduct to the west spans the Kenwyn valley and the Truro or Moresk viaduct to the east crosses the Allen valley. Seen from the top of St Clement's Hill they look like one continuous structure. With a length of 1,329 feet the Truro viaduct is the longest in Cornwall, with the Carvedras viaduct slightly shorter at just 969 feet. Like all railway viaducts in Cornwall, they were originally constructed from stone piers with the track supported on wooden trestles, but these proved expensive to maintain, and between 1902 and 1904 both viaducts were replaced with the stone arches we see today. These were constructed alongside the originals, but the piers from the old viaducts were not demolished and remain in place.

The West Cornwall railway reached Truro from Penzance in 1852 and to save money was constructed in standard gauge. The line terminated at Newham Quay (see separate entry). The Cornwall Railway's broad-gauge track arrived from Plymouth in 1859 and terminated at the main railway station which is still in use today. When the line from Penzance was connected to the new station, the different gauges meant that trains could not run through and much inconvenience to passengers ensued. This was resolved in 1866 when the West Cornwall line was converted to broad gauge.

The sixteen-arch Truro or Moresk Viaduct is the longest in Cornwall.

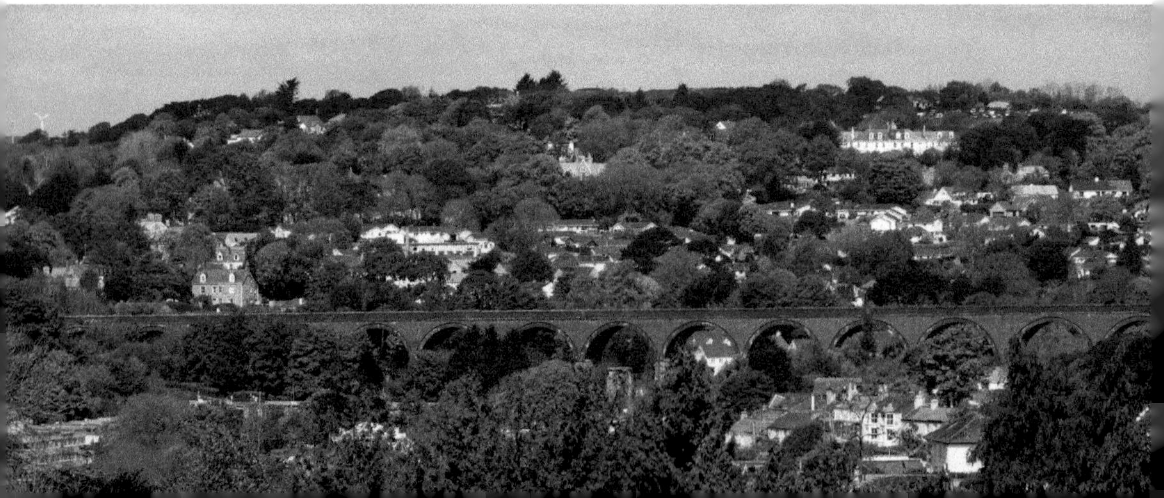

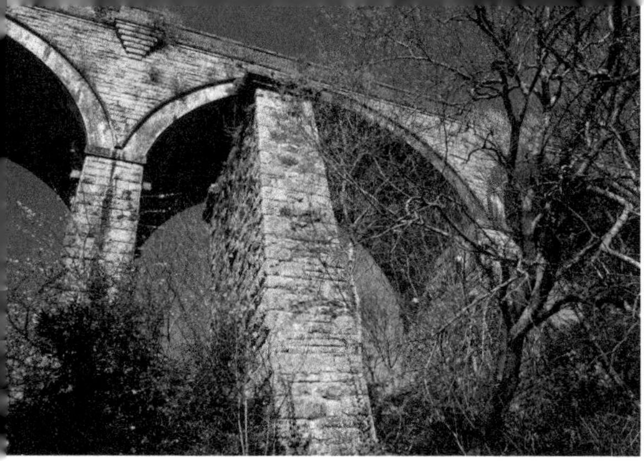
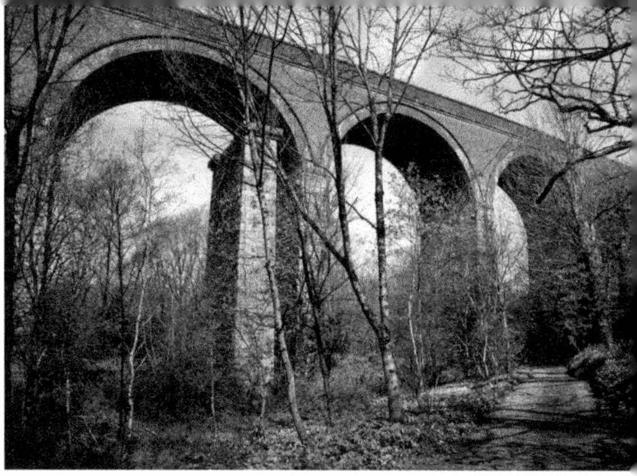

Above left: One of the old piers of the Carvedras viaduct.

Above right: The Truro or Moresk viaduct at Daubuz Moor.

They had backed the wrong horse however: the GWR, who took over the Cornwall railway in 1889, eventually decided that there was no future in broad gauge and the whole length of track through Cornwall was converted to standard gauge over a single weekend in May 1892.

Victoria Gardens

Laid out to commemorate Queen Victoria's Diamond Jubilee in 1897, these lovely gardens lie on a south-facing slope overlooking the River Kenwyn and St George's Church, to the rear of the County Court building. The ornate wrought-iron bandstand

Springtime in Victoria Gardens.

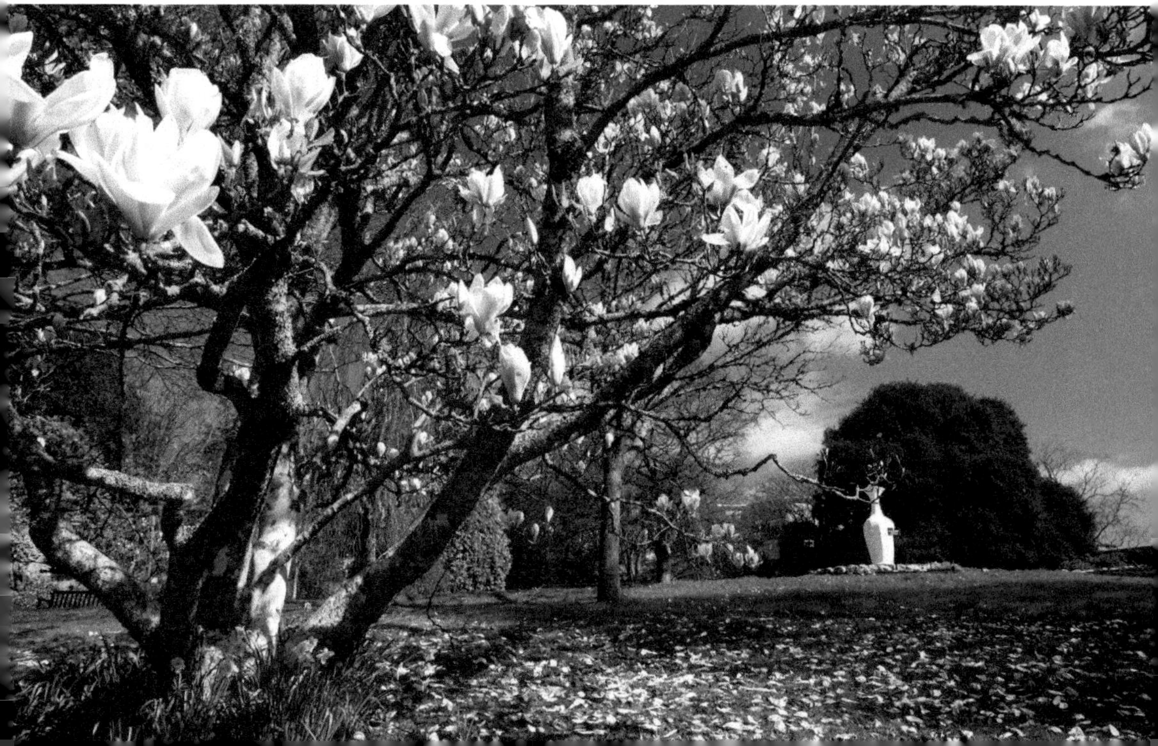

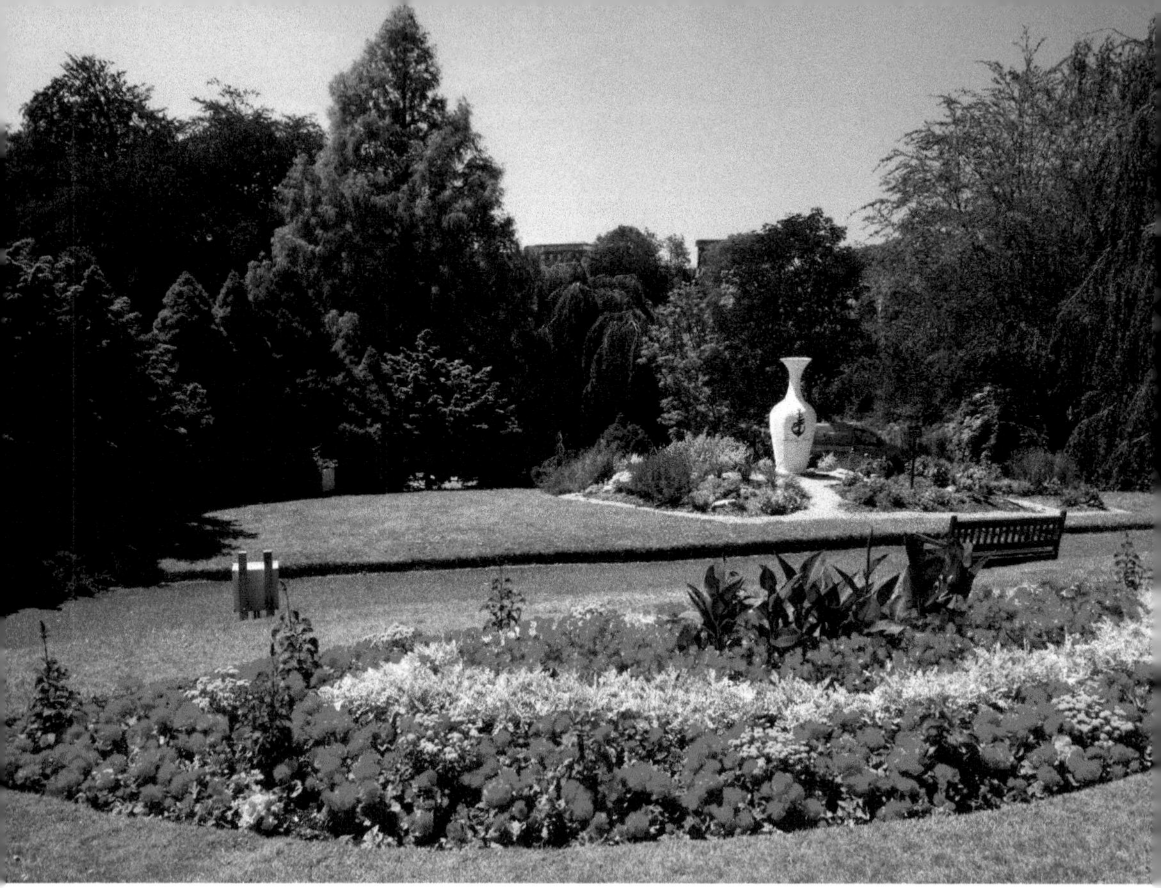

Above: The Invictus Vase of Hope in Victoria Gardens.

Below: Wrought-iron bandstand in Victoria Gardens.

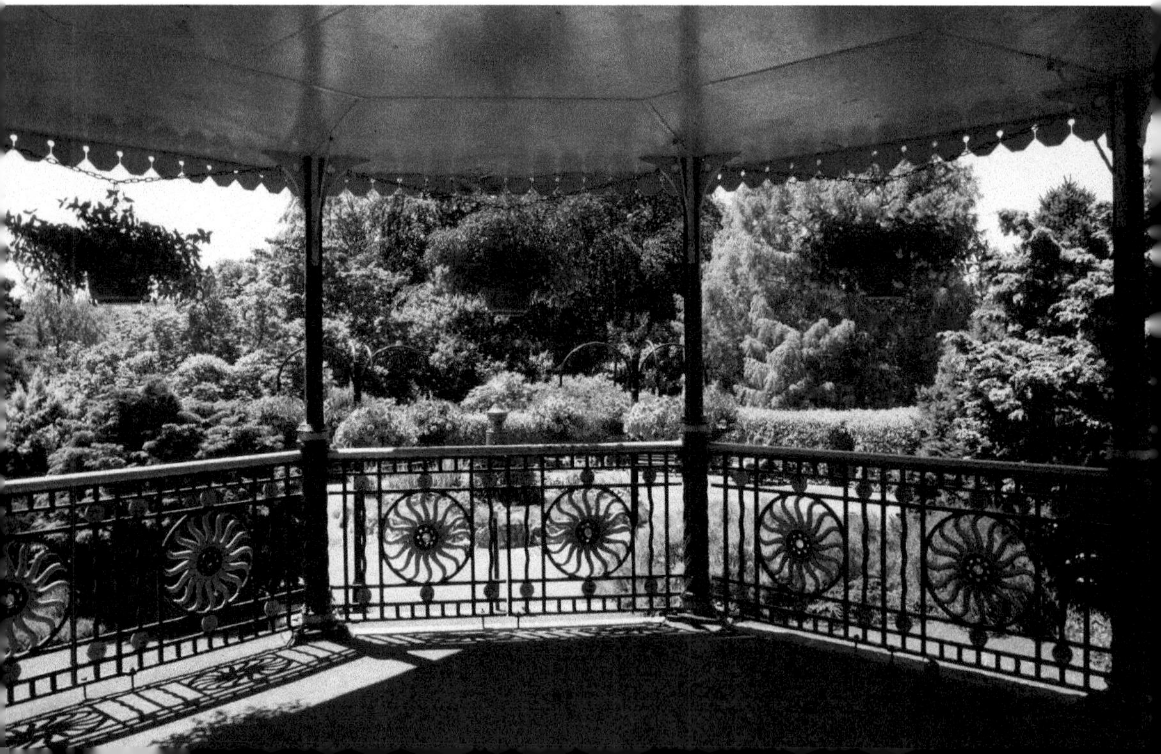

is a venue for band concerts on summer Sundays, and the fountain in front of it once stood in Boscawen Street. A recent addition, in August 2018, is the *Invictus Vase of Hope*, a sculpture by Wadebridge sculptor Richard Austen, which he produced as a result of a commission from a Middle-Eastern sheik. For human rights reasons however, Richard decided not to sell to the commissioner but instead donated the vase to the Invictus Trust.

Vivian, Richard Hussey

Decorated for his role in the Battle of Waterloo, Richard Hussey Vivian is one of Cornwall's most dashing military heroes, some say the model on which Winston Graham based his hero Ross Poldark. Born in Truro in 1775, his father was a mining magnate and vice-warden of the Stannaries who later moved to South Wales where he had extensive interests in the copper works. As a boy Richard attended Truro Grammar School under Dr Cardew, moved to Lostwithiel and then to Harrow. After attending Oxford for less than a year, he journeyed to France to complete his education. His father was keen that Richard join the family business, but his son had other ideas and after a brief period in the legal profession, in 1793 he obtained a commission in the Independent Company of Foot.

That a military career was the right one there was never any doubt; he was a natural soldier and within a year became a captain in the 28th Regiment of Foot. Serving in Flanders, by 1800 he was promoted to Major and by 1804 to Lt Colonel. He fought in the Peninsular War and by 1815 he was a Major General and received a knighthood. He commanded the 6th Brigade during Waterloo and his heroics led to him receiving more accolades, not only from his home country but also from Russia and Austria. He was given a momentous homecoming when he returned to Truro as a hero.

He married twice: his first marriage, in 1804, was to Eliza Champion, descended from a French family. The wedding took place at Gretna Green due to the disapproval of both families. The couple had five children but sadly Eliza died in 1831. He also had an illegitimate son who had been brought up as one of the family. In 1833 he married Letitia Webster and had two more children.

In 1820 he became an equerry to George IV and in 1830 Groom of the Bedchamber. After his military career ended, he became MP for Truro and later Windsor, was created a Baronet of Truro in 1828 and received a peerage in 1841, the year before he died. He suffered from heart trouble in later life and in 1842 travelled to Baden-Baden where on 20 August he died suddenly from a ruptured aneurism. His body was brought back to Truro via Falmouth and carried upriver on the paddle steamer *Dart*. It was interred in the family vault in St Mary's churchyard. On the day of his funeral all of Truro's shops closed for three hours.

W

Walsingham Place

In the fifteenth century the land on which Walsingham Place stands was a boggy area beside the River Kenwyn. By the end of the seventeenth century it had become known as Caribee, or Cribby, Island and was the home of slaves from Caribbean slave trading ships docking in Truro. With the building of Georgian Lemon Street in the early part of the nineteenth century, in 1837 MP Edmund Turner financed the building of a curved terrace on the land using plans drawn up by, it is thought, architect Philip Sambell, who went on to design Truro Savings Bank in River Street, later to become

Walsingham Place, thought to be designed by Philip Sambell.

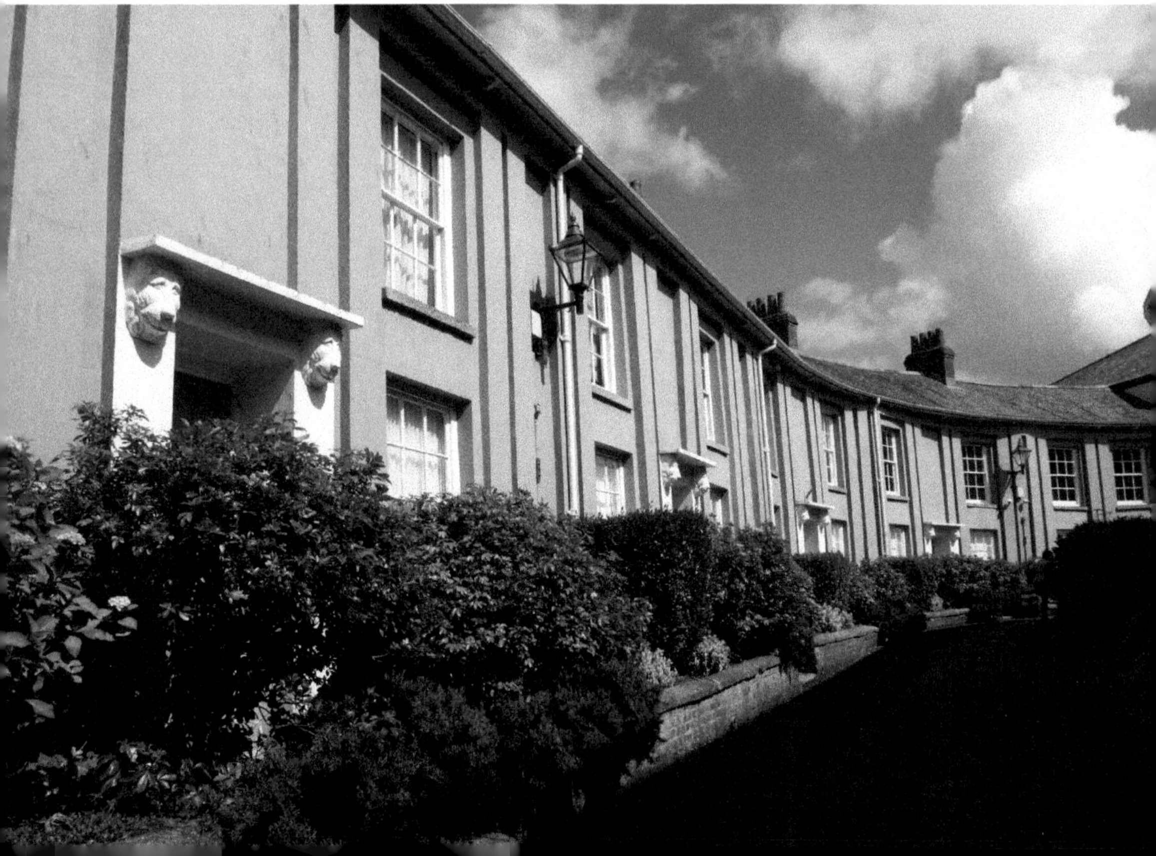

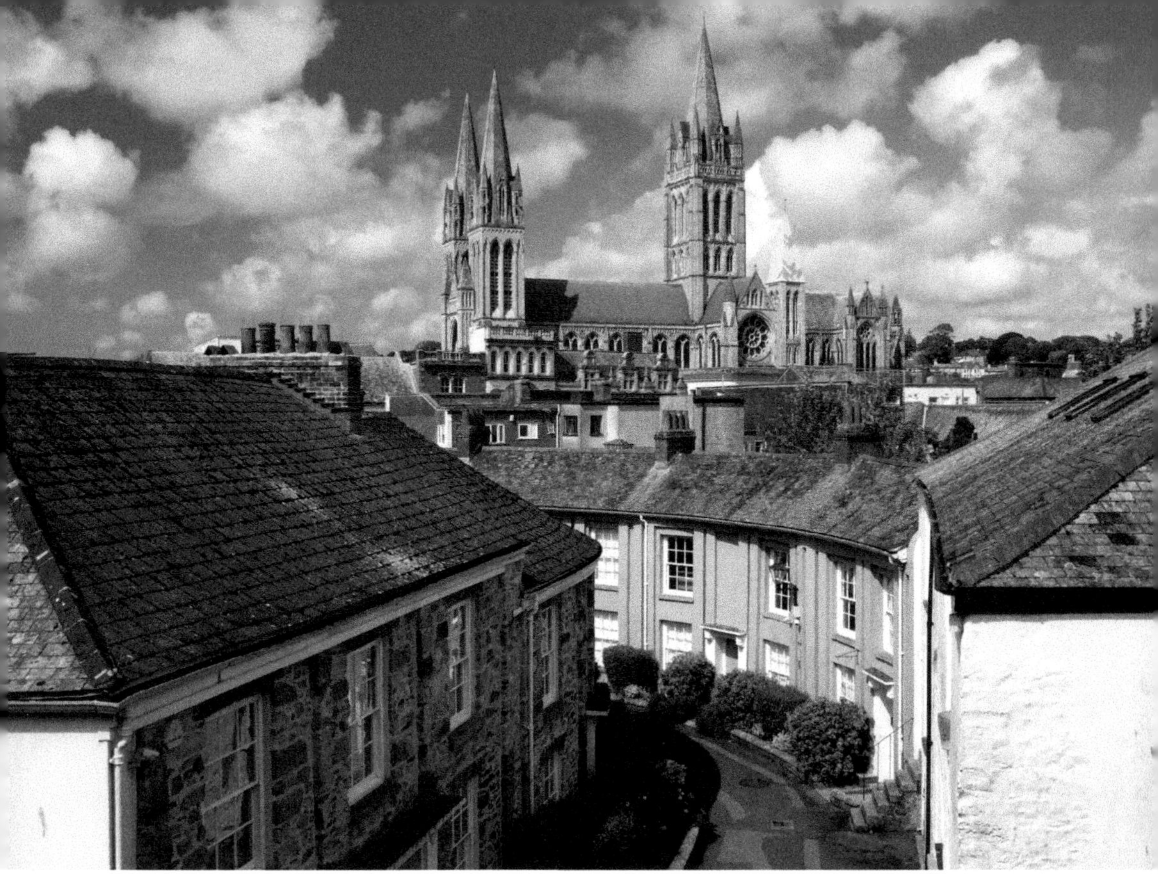

the Royal Cornwall Museum. The lions' heads that adorn each doorway were added much later, in the 1960s. Its name has no direct link with the Norfolk town, but was named after the MP's brother, Walsingham Turner. Today it is one of the most elegant streets in the city, but was very nearly demolished in the 1960s to make way for a modern development. It was saved after the intervention of Poet Laureate Sir John Betjeman, who was researching a Shell Guide to the county at the time. It now leads to a modern multi-storey car park whose decks provide an excellent bird's-eye view of the crescent against the backdrop of the cathedral.

At the end of the crescent beside the car park is an interesting building, now a delicatessen and café, which has a varied history. In the early 1800s it was a malting

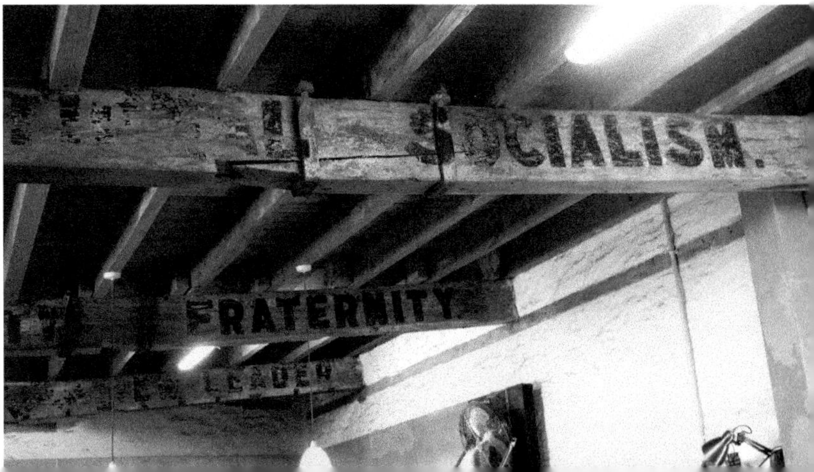

Socialist graffiti dating from the 1920s is a feature of the Cornish Food Box café in Walsingham Place.

house, and has some very deep cellars through which ran the River Kenwyn. Since then it has been used as a boxing club, dance hall, and a coffin store for Mallets next door (see separate entry). During the 1920s it became the headquarters of the Independent Labour Party and the café still displays the socialist slogans painted on the beams, which are thought to date from the National Strike of 1926.

West, Edwy Arthur

Edwy West, known as Arthur, was born near Penzance in 1875 and his family later moved to Truro where Edwy joined the cathedral choir. After leaving school he moved away to work in a furnishing store in Portsmouth, but returned in 1905 to marry a Truro girl, Ada Worth. The couple moved away to Bristol and then Bournemouth as Edwy pursued his retail career. In the meantime they had two daughters, Constance and Barbara. Edwy's wanderlust took hold and the family decided to move to Florida where Edwy planned to start a fruit business. Early in 1912 they paid £27 15*s* for a family ticket, number 34651, on the newly launched liner *RMS Titanic* and on 10 April the family, with Ada now pregnant with the couple's third child, embarked on their fateful voyage. Ada later described the events of the night of 15 April 1912:

> We were all asleep when the collision took place, but were only jolted in our berths, my husband and children not being awakened, and it was only the hurrying of passengers outside our cabin door that caused alarm. The steward bade us all get up and dressed thoroughly with plenty of warm clothes. Arthur placed lifebelts upon the children and carried them to the boat deck. I followed carrying my handbag. After seeing us safely into the lifeboat Arthur returned to the cabin for a Thermos of hot milk and finding the lifeboat let down, he reached it by means of a rope, gave the flask to me and with a farewell returned to the deck of the ship.

Ada and her family survived, but Arthur was lost. She returned to England and her home city on the White Star liner *Celtic* and in September gave birth to the couple's third daughter, who she named Edwyna Joan. Their second daughter, Barbara, who died in 2007 at the age of ninety-six, lived long enough to become the last-but-one *Titanic* survivor. Her funeral was held in the cathedral where a plaque to Edwy's memory was also placed. In all there were sixty-one passengers and crew from Cornwall aboard the *Titanic*, sixteen of whom survived, all of them female.

Father Willis

Truro Cathedral's organ was custom-built in 1887 by one of the country's finest organ builders, Henry 'Father' Willis, at a cost of £2,700. It was transported from London by boat. The blower was powered by water from the nearby millpool (see River Allen) until an electric motor was installed in the 1920s. The cathedral's first organist was George Sinclair, who later moved to Hereford and was immortalised as G. R. S. in Elgar's *Enigma Variations*. The organ was refurbished in 1963 under the supervision of the builder's grandson, also called Henry Willis. One long-overdue improvement was to move the organ loft from its position 36 feet up in the main case, a climb of some thirty steps up a spiral staircase, which George Sinclair used to run up two at a time. Father Willis believed that the organist should be both fit and close to the action! A number of aids were installed in order that the organist could see and talk to the choir far below: there was an arrangement of five mirrors, a speaking tube, and an ingenious system of red lights, one flash for play, two for stop playing, and three to inform the organist they were playing the wrong hymn! Inevitably, there was the occasional accidental fumble with the manuscript resulting in a sheaf of papers falling down on the choir below! One organist would take his typewriter up there and catch up with his paperwork during the sermon!

The loft is now repositioned in the south transept nearer the choir, making it much easier for the organist to see and hear the choir they are supposed to be accompanying. After a further refurbishment in 1991, the organ still sounds as good, or perhaps better, than when it was built, and is numbered among the six finest in Europe. You can listen to it at one of the free weekly lunchtime organ recitals given by guest organists during the summer.

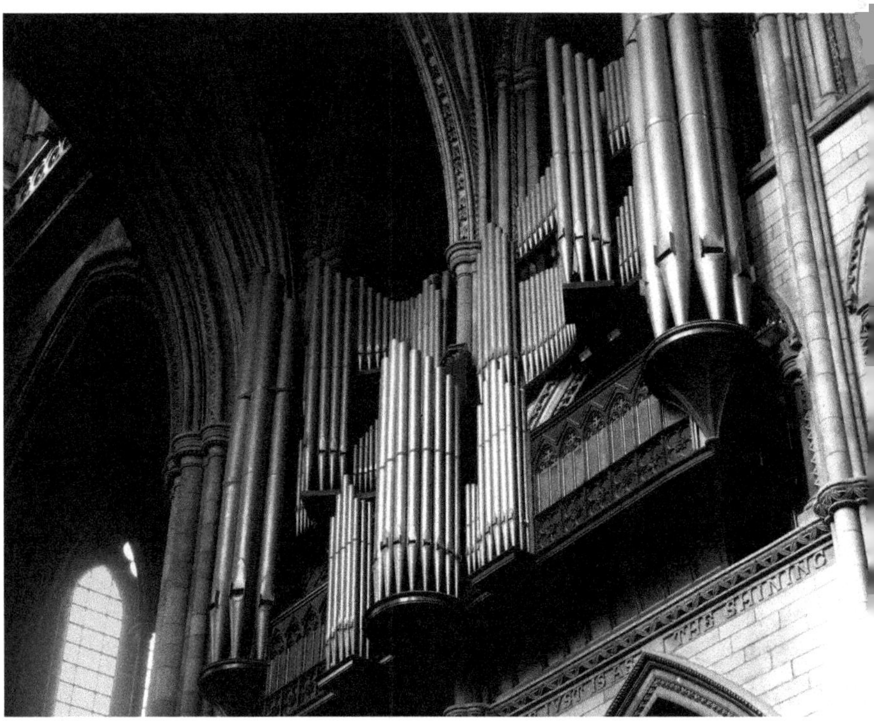

The Father Willis organ in Truro Cathedral.

X

Xmas Carols

Truro was the location of an ecclesiastical first in 1880. The first Bishop of Truro, Dr Edward White Benson, later to become Archbishop of Canterbury, devised a service of lessons and carols which was to begin at 10 p.m. on Christmas Eve. In fact, the idea was not his, but had been suggested to him by his succentor, Somerset Walpole, who later became Bishop of Edinburgh. Benson decided on nine lessons, the first of which was to be read by a junior chorister, then continuing up through the hierarchy of the cathedral, with the final reading by Benson himself. Carols were becoming popular by

Truro Cathedral at Christmas.

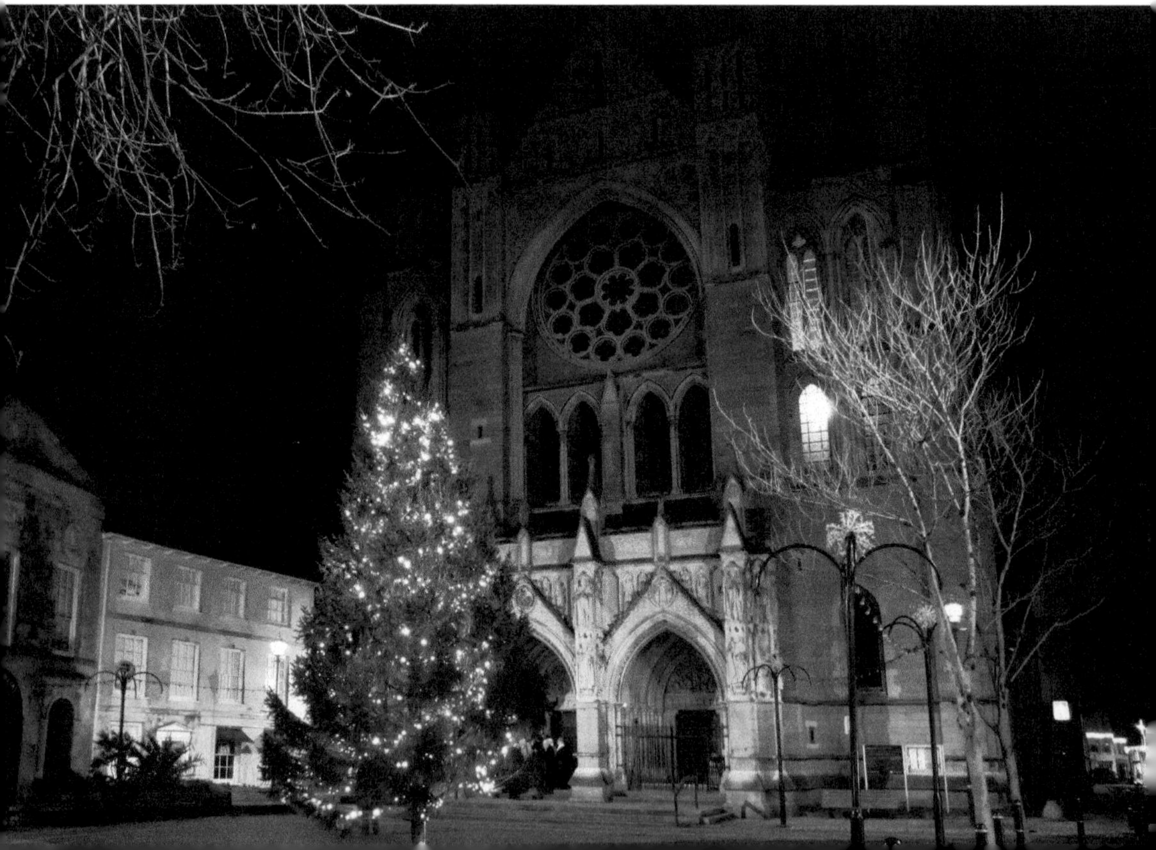

the late Victorian era, and Benson used a collection called *Christmas Carols New and Old*, a copy of which, together with the original order of service, is kept in Cornwall's record office. These saw the light of day once more on 17 November 2013, when the present choir under the direction of Christopher Gray led a reconstruction of the service. The major difference was actually the building itself: the cathedral was still unfinished in 1880 and the first service took place in the temporary wooden building which for seven years stood in as Truro's first cathedral. That building was eventually moved a few miles away to Redruth where it became Smith's Cathedral Boot Works until it was destroyed by a fire in 1981. The service of Nine Lessons and Carols quickly spread around the world and most famously to King's College Cambridge, where it was first held, with a few innovations, in 1918.

Xmas Primestock Show

Described as the day the country comes to town, the present Fatstock Show began in the old cattle market in 1902, although a smaller show had been held for some years previously. By the 1980s it had moved to the new cattle market on the western edge of the city, and in line with changing tastes, changed its name to the Primestock Show. In 2002, the event moved back into the city centre, occupying the piazza on Lemon Quay, and to celebrate, Mr Edward Carlyon, the City Coroner and a freeman of the city, exercised his right to drive a flock of sheep through the streets accompanied by the bishop and mayor. Today it is believed to be the only Christmas cattle show held in the centre of a UK city.

Judging Red Devons at Truro's Primestock Show.

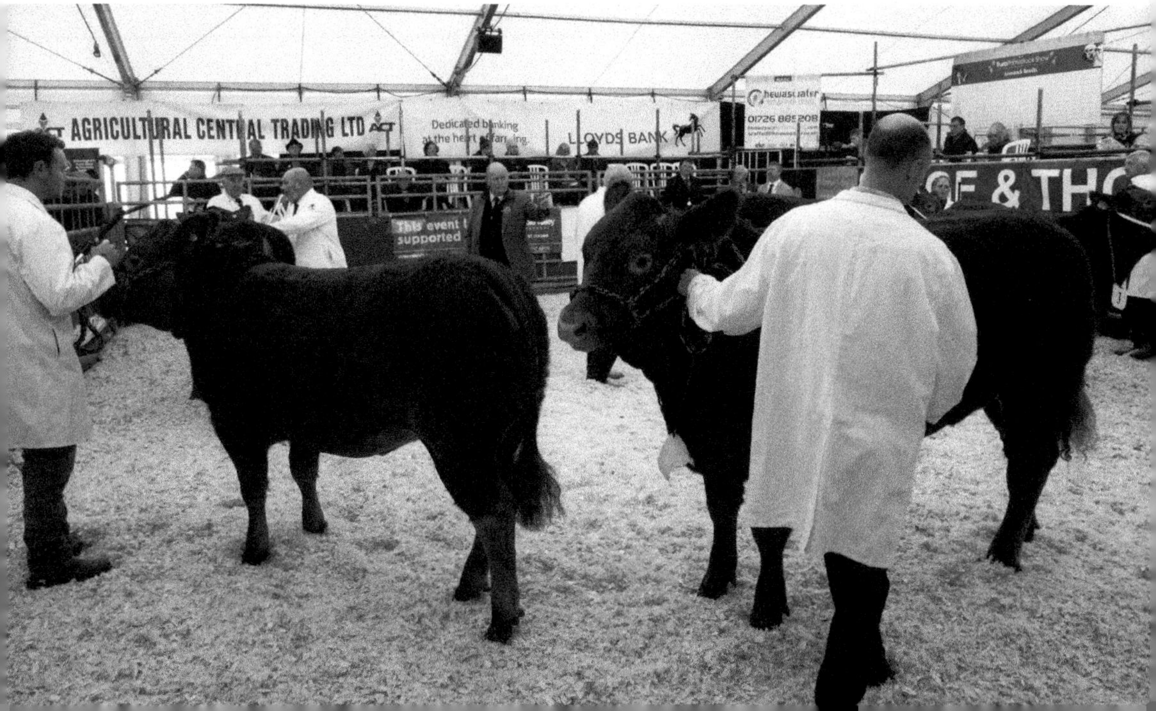

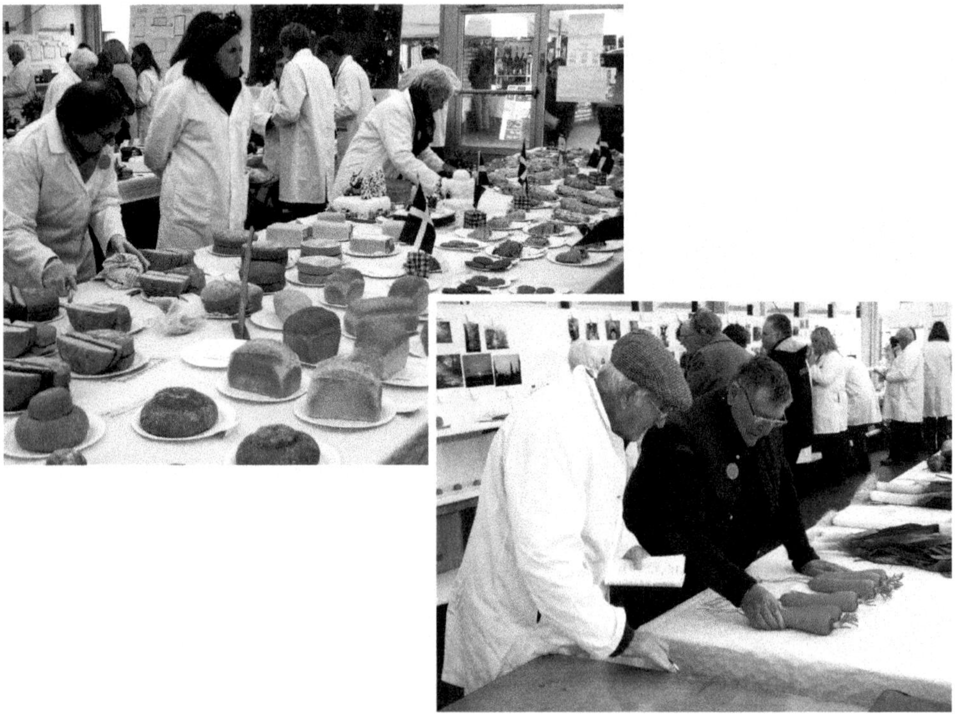

Judges discuss baking and vegetable exhibits at the Primestock Show.

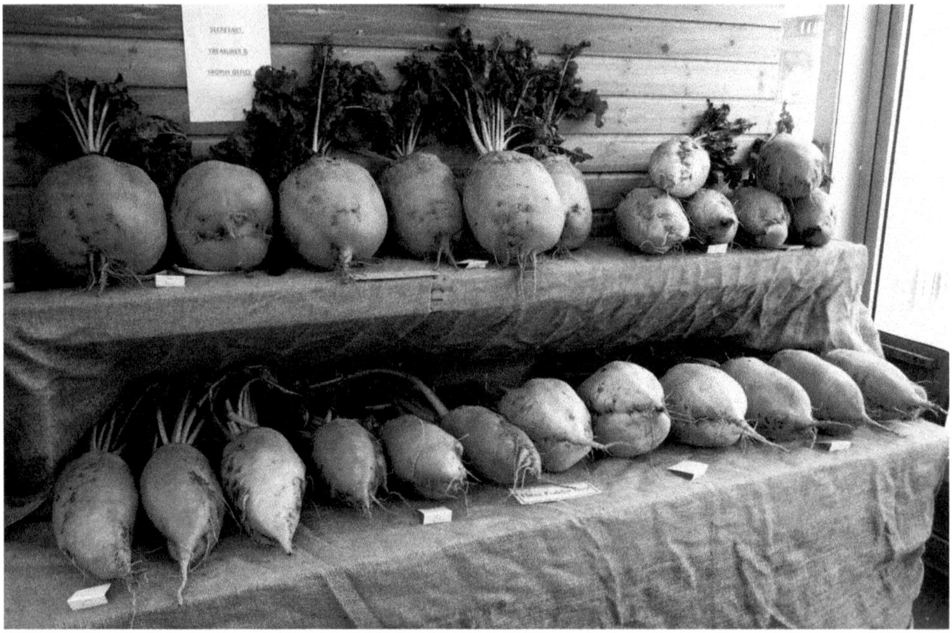

A display of mangel-wurzels at the Primestock Show.

Y

Yew Tree Court

In 2000, the Yew Tree Court development of the old Union Workhouse site off Tregolls Road won an award from an architecture journal for best regeneration scheme in the South West. Seventy-five mews houses and apartments were created around a beautiful central garden in a building that was once the city's former workhouse.

Truro has had several workhouses since the first was built in 1743. Overcrowding soon led to the need for a larger one, which was built in 1779, while Kenwyn had its own workhouse. In 1829 the parish of St Clements built a new workhouse at the top of St Clement's Hill. In 1850, following the Poor Law Union of 1834, a new Union

Yew Tree Court, once Truro's Union Workhouse.

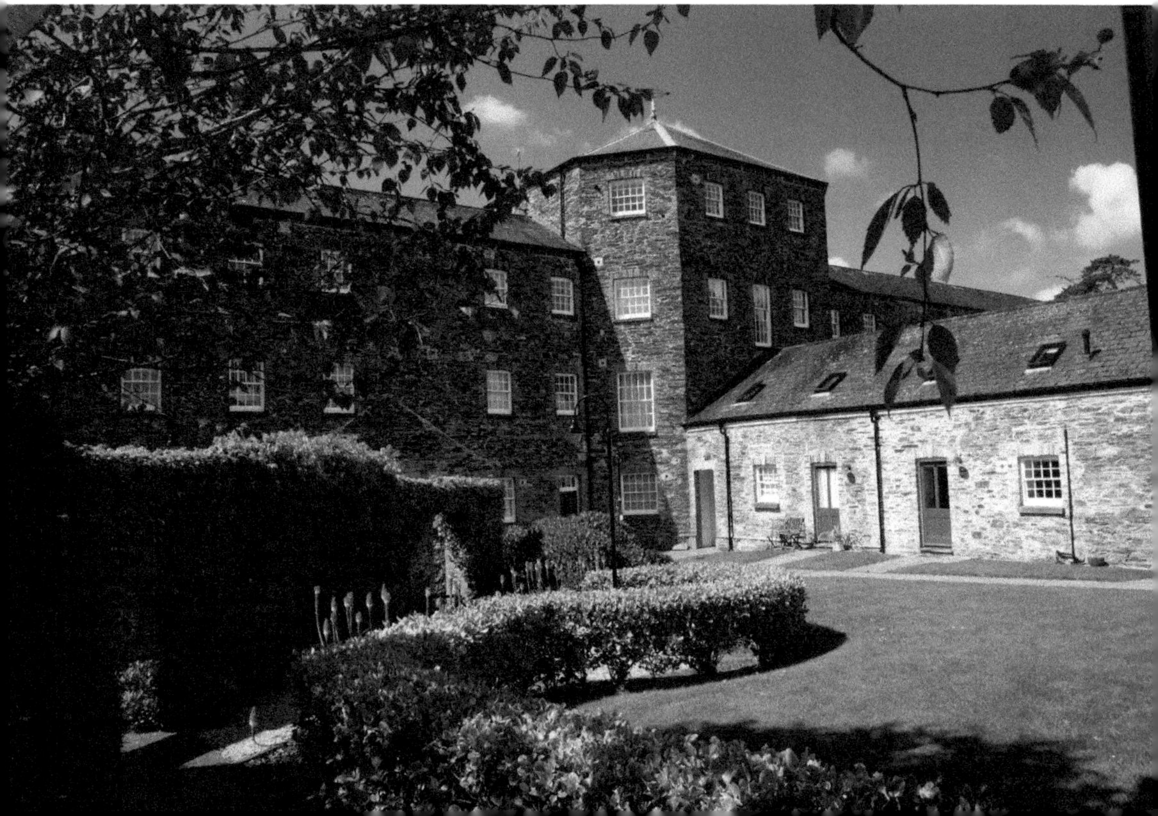

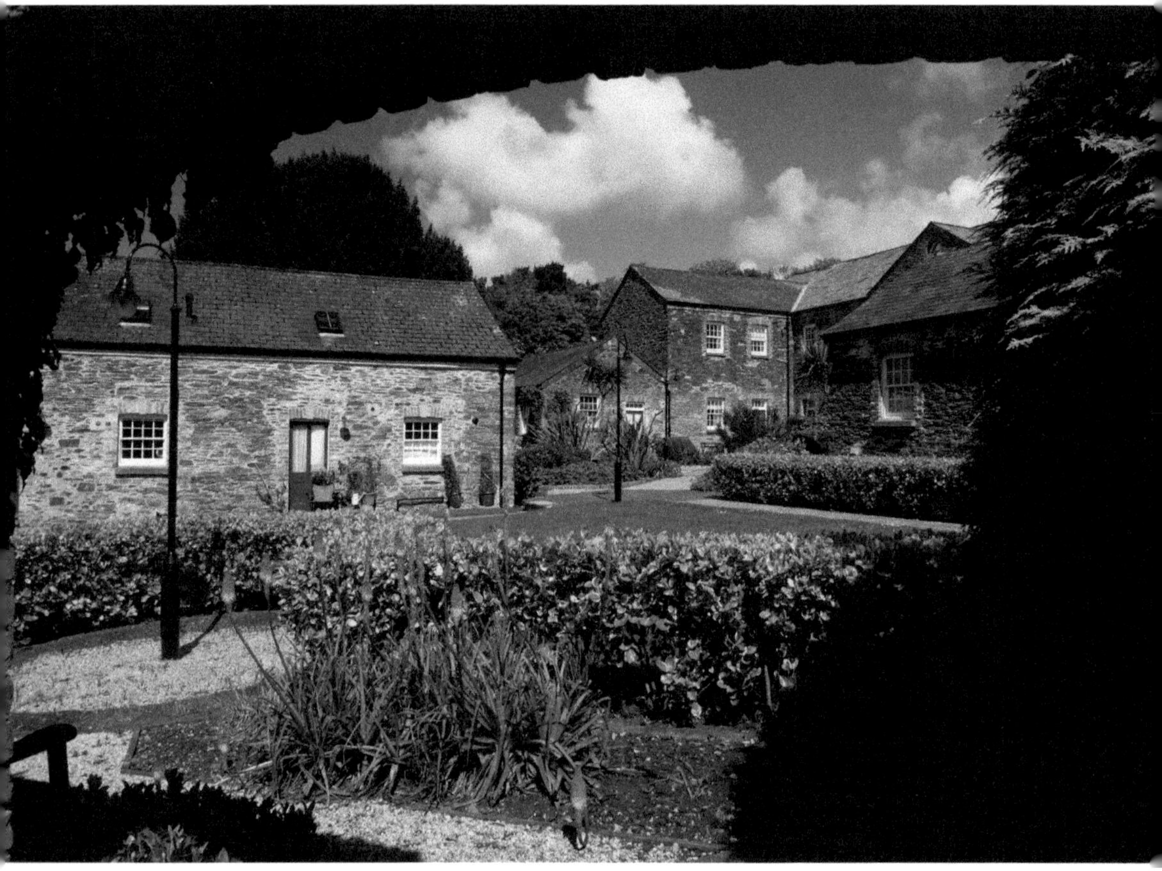

workhouse was built at the top of what is today Tregolls Road, at the north-eastern end of the city. The building was designed by William Harris and followed a cruciform plan. It cost £12,196 to build. There was an entrance archway and a central hub from which various accommodation wings extended. An infirmary block with seventy-eight beds and an isolation block were also built. An inspection of the infirmary on behalf of the British Medical Journal in 1894 revealed much which needed improvement, including a lack of hot water and a shortage of staff. During the First World War the inmates were temporarily boarded elsewhere and the infirmary became the Truro Auxiliary Naval Hospital. They returned after the war and the management was taken over by Cornwall County Council in 1929. During the Second World War the site became an isolation hospital and with the birth of the NHS after the war became St Clements Hospital. A new hospital was built at Treliske in the 1960s and in 1974 the site became an administrative centre for the Area Health Authority before being sold for residential development.

Z

Z

In 1847 Prime Minister Lord John Russell stated in parliament that he was considering nominating a bishop for Cornwall, possibly based in Bodmin. A correspondent to the *Royal Cornwall Gazette*, using the pseudonym 'Z', vigorously opposed the choice of Bodmin, including its lack of a main-line railway connection (Bodmin was on a branch line) and putting forward the argument that the church building in Bodmin could be less easily enlarged to provide a cathedral than St Mary's in Truro. A further argument 'Z' expounded was that Bodmin had taken part in the so-called surplice riots of 1844, opposing the edict put forward by Bishop Philpotts that clergy should wear surplices when preaching, at the time considered a high-church cathedral-like practice.

Zealotry

When Bishop Benson was appointed as the first Bishop of Truro, nonconformist Edward Fish wrote in the *Royal Cornwall Gazette* that the people of Cornwall needed a bishop about as much as a duck needed an umbrella. The arrival of John Wesley in the county in the mid-eighteenth century began this nonconformist zeal with many chapels being built to satisfy the spiritual needs of the miners who felt left out by the Anglican Church. However, in Truro, the most zealous of preachers occupied the pulpit of none other than the Anglican St Mary's Parish Church in the town, later to become the cathedral. When the Revd Samuel Walker took up the curacy of St Mary's in 1746, it was said that he was more concerned with learning to dance than preaching the gospel, but this soon changed as a result of his friendship with George Conon, headmaster of Truro Grammar School. Walker experienced a conversion and began to take his preaching duties very seriously, building up a large congregation of like-minded followers. On a number of occasions, he refused to officiate at the funerals of those he saw as unrepentant transgressors, and was subsequently disciplined by the bishop. His version of the gospel became quite extreme and he considered the

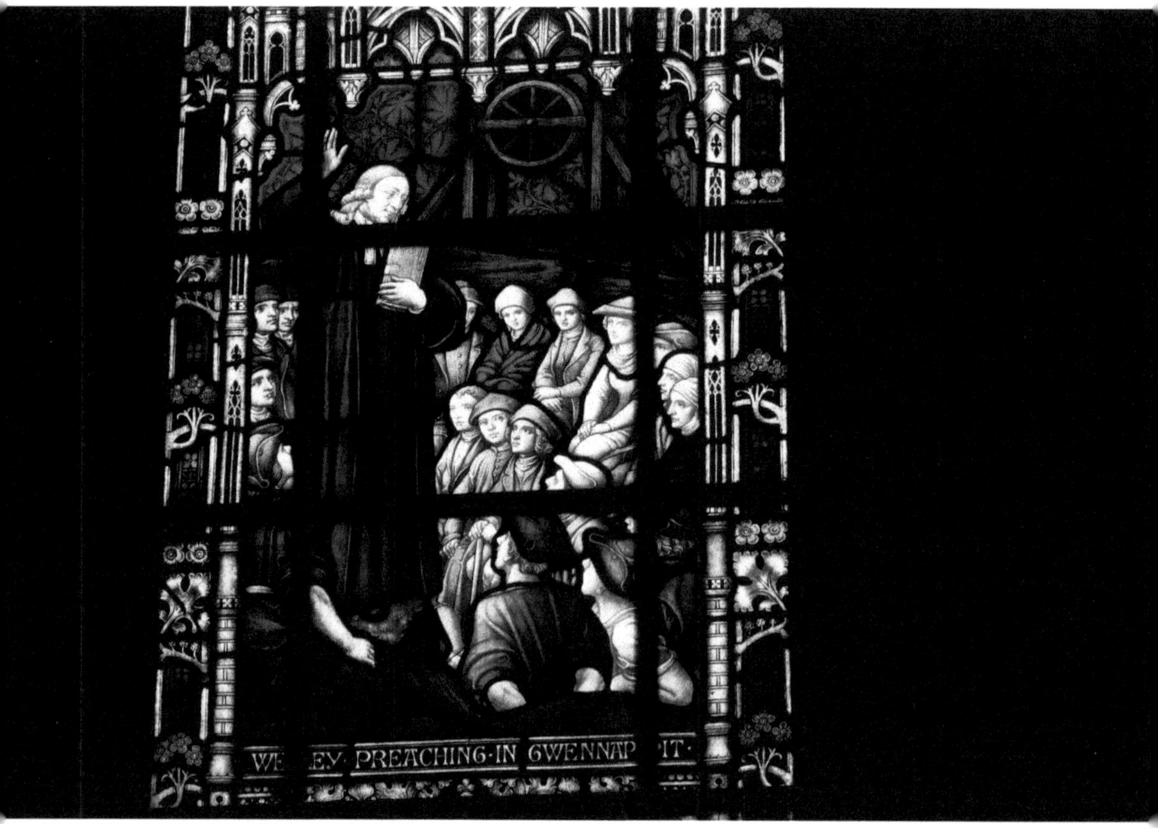

Stained glass showing John Wesley preaching in Cornwall, Truro Cathedral.

preaching of John Wesley to be too lenient. Out of respect for his views, Wesley did not preach in Truro until after Walker's death in 1761. He visited Truro several times after that, the last time in 1789. Both Wesley and Walker agreed on their loyalty to the Anglican Church, not wishing for their followers to leave it, but Walker did not approve of travelling preachers. After he died most of his congregation left to form their own meeting when his successor at St Mary's, the Revd Charles Pye, famously announced that his pulpit 'so stinks of Calvinism that not a century will purge it'. In 1769 Walker's congregation began to meet in a disused cockpit building at the end of what is today The Leats. Previously known as 'Walkerites', they now acquired a new nickname of 'Cockpitarians'.

Bibliography

Barham, Fisher, *The Creation of a Cathedral* (Falmouth: Glasney Press, 1976).

Farmer, David, *The Warrior of the West: Richard Hussy Vivian* (Llandybie: Cyhoeddwyr Dinefwr Publishers, 2005).

Graves, Laura, *Thomas Varker Keam, Indian Trader* (Norman: University of Oklahoma Press, 1998).

Jameson, Bernadette, *The Boy Who Played His Way to Freedom* (Lulu.com, 2012).

Kittridge, Alan, *Passenger Steamers of the River Fal* (Truro: Twelveheads, 1988).

McGrady, Richard, *Music and Musicians in Early Nineteenth Century Cornwall* (University of Exeter, 1991).

Miller, David, *The Episcopate of Bishop Benson 1877–1883 and the beginnings of Truro Diocese and Cathedral: The Umbrella and the Duck* (University of Exeter, PhD Thesis, 2012).

Mudd, David, *About the City* (St Teath: Bossiney Books, 1979).

Parnell, Christine, *The Book of Truro* (Tiverton: Halsgrove, 2004).

Parnell, Christine, *Truro in 50 Buildings* (Stroud: Amberley Publishing, 2018).

Richards, Paul, *Francis Guillaume Ormond: The Life of a 'Cornish' Musician* (1994).

Rowe, Ashley, *The Truro Ghost and other Cornish Ghost Stories* (Monmouth: Oakmagic Publications, 2003; first published 1941).

Sambells, Frank, *Philip Sambell Jr. An Architect of his Time* (Winnipeg: Art Bookbindery, 2018).

Tonkin, Ronald, *Traders of Bygone Truro* (self-published, 1986).

Tregallas, Walter, *Cornish Worthies, Vol. I* (London: Elliot Stock, 1884).

White, Rupert, *Queen in Cornwall* (Antenna Publications, 2011).

Acknowledgements

I am grateful to Jenny Stephens of Amberley Publishing for her editorial guidance. Most of the photographs reproduced in this book are my own, and I thank all the property owners for permission to reproduce those taken at privately owned locations, namely Abby Keverne (The Alverton), Liz Mulloy (Truro Cathedral), Fr John Gilbert (Our Lady of the Portal and St Piran), Wendy Perry (Bosvigo), Revd Elizabeth Wild (St Endellion), Lucy Jones (The Cornish Food Box Co.), Tanya Thomas (Truro Primestock Show), and Martin Foy (Yew Tree Court). Yvonne Hollyoak of Proper Cornish allowed me to photograph their Furniss tin collection, Amanda Hawkins of Showpiece Antiques supplied the picture of a Percy's Pectoral Balsam bottle, and Dr Jan Knight of Park Pharmacy Trust allowed me to photograph her Percy's Rennet bottles. Bert Biscoe, city councillor, Michael Tedder (Epiphany House), Rupert White and Philip Hosken provided invaluable help on points of detail.

About the Author

John Husband grew up in the Cornish village of Gorran Haven and has lived all his life in the county. He has spent his career in the clay industry, has a PhD in Paper Science from the University of Manchester and is a Fellow of the Technical Association of the Paper Industry and a member of the Royal Society of Chemistry. A self-taught photographer and writer, he has written articles for *The Lady*, *The Countryman*, *This England*, *Evergreen* and *The People's Friend.*